MONSTER-MOBILES

Barry Brazier

ISBN 0 85429 594 1

A **FOULIS** Motoring Book

First published 1987

© Barry J. Brazier 1987

Published by
Haynes Publishing Group,
Sparkford, Near Yeovil, Somerset
BA22 7JJ, England

Haynes Publications Inc.
861 Lawrence Drive, Newbury
Park, California 91320 USA

British Library Cataloguing in Publication Data

Brazier, Barry J. Monstermobiles —— (A Foulis
    motoring book).
    1. Trucks —— United States
    I. Title
    629.2'24'0973   TL230

    ISBN 0-85429-594-1

Library of Congress catalog card number 87-81362

Editor: Mansur Darlington

Layout design: Chris Hull

Printed in England by: J. H. Haynes & Co. Ltd.

CONTENTS

FOREWORD
by Robert 'Bob' Chandler

WHAT IS *BIGFOOT?* WHERE DID YOU GET the idea for *BIGFOOT?* How many times I've been asked those questions! *BIGFOOT* came into being as one of a line of family pleasure and work trucks. One of the very best things about trucks, is that they are true family vehicles and off-roading is a recreation that is fun, exciting, and family oriented. Whether you camp in your truck, bring a tent, or sleep in the bed of the truck, you can join the great pastime of getting away from it all. What better way to be with your family, let them commune with nature, be on their own? You can even let the kids drive. When I ordered a new 1974 F-250, little did I know what fame was in store for my new Ford. I had experimented with my other vehicles, even building up a home business with like-minded enthusiasts and still playing on the weekend. This vehicle became special. First came larger tires, then wheels, then a bigger engine followed by bigger axles. The time came when I'd pull into a filling station and people would gather around to see the truck.

I spent more time working on other people's vehicles. The garage was full of equipment. The time was ripe for a move into bigger quarters, and a regular business. I took a leave of absence from my carpentry job, but never returned. Midwest Four Wheel Drive Center, Inc. was born, and my truck, now named *BIGFOOT,* matured.

As *BIGFOOT* evolved, it became a business unto itself. Gradually, the weekend camping trips changed to weekend races. We participated in mud runs, truck pulls, sand drags, and hillclimbs. You name it, and we went to it, at first on our own and then at the request of the promoters.

As the sport of off-roading grew in popularity, so did *BIGFOOT*-it was unique.

BIGFOOT embodied that elusive star quality; people were drawn to it. I can't explain why. I only know it's so. With the help of extensive media coverage, it became a phenomenon worthy of imitation.

By the late seventies, *BIGFOOT* was travelling full time, and by 1982 a second *BIGFOOT* came into being, creating an industry-wide impact when it appeared with huge 66-inch tires and spawning a new being–the 'Monster Truck'. *BIGFOOT III, IV, V, Ms, The Aerostar,* and now *BIGFOOT VI* followed over the years, brought about by the monster truck craze that has swept the nation.

What had been a hobby turned into a full-time career. I think this happened to a lot of 4-wheel drive and off-road enthusiasts in the late 70s. What started out as personal recreation, grew into the business of off-roading, and what was a personal participant hobby, ended up being 'Off-road Motorsports' which became a full fledged sport.

While there's still the fun, the personal pleasure and the satisfaction of building something unique that started a trend, don't think any motor sport is just fun. There is a lot of work involved. It's a big commitment and you end up living, breathing, eating and sleeping your business. Ask any truck or tractor puller, any off-road racer.

You have to keep ahead, always be new and fresh. 'He who doesn't go forward, goes backwards', has always been my motto. When we first did a car crush, we were unsure, thinking it might be deemed destructive and unwholesome.

It was almost six months after our first crush, that we finally did a car crush before an audience. The results were amazing–no negative reaction, but a crowd that loved it. They stood and cheered. Another milestone in the legend of *BIGFOOT.*

I've been lucky, *BIGFOOT* has always been a family venture. Marilyn and our children are as much part of this story as I am. I couldn't have done it without the help of numerous other people along the way, particularly the fans, and especially the kids. They are some of *BIGFOOT's* biggest fans and our best assets. Just to see the look in their eyes, the sparkle and gleam of their smiles and the excitement in their bodies as they sit on the edge of their seats watching *BIGFOOT* makes it all worthwhile.

Truck pulling, *BIGFOOT,* the monster truck phenomenon; these have all helped trucks to outsell cars for the first time ever in America, and have raised the lowly pickup truck to the status vehicle of today.

Robert 'Bob' Chandler
Hazelwood, Missouri

ACKNOWLEDGEMENTS by the Author

MOTORSPORTS ARE A TEAM EFFORT; therefore, a book on the subject of off-road motorsports must also be a team effort. When this project began, I had little idea of where to start, or who to work with. Connie Hohman, Sheri Johnson and Cindy Landes of SRO, helped with the times and places of their nationwide event schedules. Don Gillespie, the editor of the NTPA's monthly newspaper, *The Puller,* not only gave much research materials, but also delved into the photo files to find some vintage NTPA. Thanks also to the folks at Special Events, Inc. for the fall Jamboree. Much gratitude must go to Bob and Marilyn Chandler and Jim Kramer for their friendship, time and free exchange of some of the photos that have never been seen outside of their own magazine, *Bigfoot, The Living Legend.* Thanks must also go to Everett Jasmer of *USA-1,* Fred Shafer of Bear Foot, Inc. and the Spiker family, for the privilege of using their photos. For a few hours aid in editing, I must thank Dennis Adler.

For those men that make these sports a family affair, you know how many hours it takes to prepare and be ready to compete as well as the number of days away from the family. Thanks to my wife, Pat, for such understanding.

Photography accomplished with Olympus camera equipment, using Fuji 35mm color slide film.

1

1 Hot – Rodders & Homebuilts

AMERICA: A NATION ON WHEELS! THE birthplace of hot rods, little duece coupes, lead sleds, woodies, cruisin', drive-ins, muscle cars, rat motors, wide weenies, dual quads, blowers, wheelie bars and hundreds of other descriptive words that compose the language of the performance officionado, both young and old.

Inspected closely, the unique off-road competition vehicles that are portrayed in this book are a natural extension of more than automotive interests, leisure activities and the love of high performance auto sports. They have their roots deep in the heartland of the American Midwest, in the back roads of the farming communities and their county fairs.

An area that encompasses some 3.5 million square miles, the USA has as many varied terrains as there are varied interests of its inhabitants. With terrain that varies from the lowest and highest points in North America and hundreds of thousands of square miles of deserts, mountains and forests, the interest in off-road and 4x4 vehicles was a natural. So natural, in fact, that the US is host to several of the biggest names in off-road auto races: the Pikes Peak Hillclimb, the Baja 1000 (on Mexican soil, originated and sanctioned by SCORE, a US organization), the Mint 400 in Las Vegas and the Olympus International Rally in Washington state.

Some of the roots of off-roading can be traced back to the days of the original dune buggie, a specially-built glassfiber body on a VW frame, some of which were very exotic in how they were powered!

Desert racing had its infant days in the early 1960s when the US automakers were infatuated with large cubic inch engines and how they performed in drag races. Back then the only real off-road vehicle was the Jeep, a son of the World War II army go-anywhere personnel carrier. It was men Like Mickey Thompson, Parnelli Jones, Walker Evans, Bill Stroppe and (sometimes faceless) countless others that aided the fledgling off-road racing sport that started taking hold in the late 60s.

About the time off-road racing reached its public acceptance in the late 60s, the years of the Detroit 'horsepower wars' were numbered. By 1973 almost all autos had anti-pollution devices and the asphalt-tearing power of large cubic inch engines like the L-88, 440 Hemi and 429 'shotgun' were relegated to drag strips and boat racing.

About this time, the import trucks from Japan were making solid impressions upon America's youth. The off-road era had arrived–with a vengeance! The growth of off-road racing sports and entertainments made a rapid growth in the 70s with the debut of events like Mickey Thompson's Off-Road Championship Grand Prix. The forming of major sanctioning bodies like NTPA, USHRA, SCORE, HDRA and regional associations that would govern the safety of the sports future also gave credence to the off-road racers and their interests.

As off-road activities became more interesting to the populace, the truck was elevated from its former position of hauling cargo and 'Cowboy Cadillac' (as the Texan's call it), to its new found position, of almost every family considering the purchase of a truck as everyday transportation. After all, a truck could carry the ATV, motorcycle or tow the dune buggie to where they were legal to drive.

So popular has the truck become that in 1986 some 4.6 million US and foreign-built trucks were sold from a total of approximately 11 million total in US vehicle sales. Estimates say that three in ten American families own at least one truck. As these sales figures indicate, the truck is not only useful, it's also fashionable in its utilitarian abilities. As the saying goes 'It's as American as Hot Dogs, Baseball and Apple Pie'.

*The first truck the Chandler family owned, a
'67 Ford with white-spoke steel wheels and a
few other items from their burgeoning first
store . . .*

*. . . has developed into an industry. Although
Bigfoot 4x4, Inc., is now an eight truck fleet,
it's just part of an estimated 100-plus trucks that
have attained 'monster truck' status.*

II
The 1970s —
coming of age

BY THE MID 70S THE INTEREST IN off-road sports entertainment was reaching a large national audience. As the interest in tractor/truck pulling grew, so did the associations that were to guide it. The NTPA was well into a growth pattern, having established the 4x4 truck pulling class in 1976. Several small promoters had held regional events in the tractor pulling field, and the USHRA had come into being. A diversification of SRO Promotions, Inc., the USHRA/SRO folks have become the largest sanctioning body of monster truck/mud bogs/pulling/thrill shows in the world. With their announcement of a joint venture with Pace Motorsports, they hope to entertain more than six million people at over 150 indoor/stadium shows in 1987.

About the time off-road sports like those of the NTPA and USHRA were growing to national attention, the birth of another facet of off-roading was taking place in St. Louis, Missouri. Bob and Marilyn Chandler and their crew at Midwest Four Wheel Drive were putting the first set of military axles and rear steering capabilities under their '74 Ford truck. Soon after the first appearance of *Bigfoot,* there were those that quickly followed Chandler's lead into what can now be called an industry of its own, as there are those companies that actually build monster trucks as a business. The sales of those huge tires (mostly Goodyear brand) are enough to keep the doors of one business open weekly! What started as dares, challenges and the need to explore further into the outback, has grown into a multi-million dollar industry annually with toys for kids, model kits, assorted collectibles and a plethora of paraphernalia. Even TV appearances, music videos, major movies and advertising commercials have featured pulling and monster trucks.
A few of the advances that these vehicles have made over the last year or two include:
–The building of a Bigfoot-type truck for a European company.
–The appearance of tractor/truck pulling in South America.
–The formation of the World Pulling International (WPI) association to sanction world-wide pulling competitions.
–And rumors of a monster truck/truck and tractor puller tour that may take place in Europe in 1988.
There is no doubt that tractor/truck pulling and monster trucks are as uniquely American as The Statue of Liberty or The Grand Canyon. However, several questions exist today about the future of these

▶

With a history dating back some fifty years, the modified tractors came into their own in the early 70s. The simple tractor with a V-8 engine and 'platform frame' . . .

recreations: are they sport or entertainment?; present interest of a few, or future interest of many; and what's the next plateau for monster truck stunts? Although these questions can only be fully answered by time and those that have an active part in these industries, it's very apparent that tractor and truck pulling are here to stay. The growth of the NTPA and its associate of WPI bear out that this interest is no longer just American either, as 'pulls' have been staged in several countries worldwide. There is no doubt that pulling will shortly become a major interest for television sports programming as its growth seems to be never-ending. It won't be long before sanctioned pulls will be coming to Europe, as this is one of the first breakthrough markets anticipated for this sport.
As for the monster trucks, that's a little more difficult to answer briefly. Drawing on the interviews with several of the major and minor names in the field, we've come to a consensus that they will be around for some years, as people like the size, noise, car crushing and competitive racing that has lately been the format for these trucks. The format for these trucks seems to grow more demanding daily, especially now that actual side-by-side obstacle course racing is part of the show at major stadium events. Safety for spectators and drivers alike is gaining more attention at each event, and so it should. As have teams in

the past, several of the teams would like a uniform set of rules, if not an association of truck owners that would set some. As other major national and international sports have found from major injuries during competition, the safer the track and vehicles, the longer the sport will last. As Mickey Thompson (he who brought desert racing to the millions) found out some years ago, if you cannot bring the spectators to your track, then you must build the track where everyone can easily come to you. Stadium or arena off-road sports are not just the fad of today but 'the sport of the 80s' as one truck owner put it. As to whether these vehicles are sport or entertainment; Mike Hoff, NHRA veteran and top-rated funny-car/tractor puller gave us this basis for definition: 'Anytime I compete I consider that a sport'.

▲

. . . has given way to the fire-belching, ground-pounding, deafening multiple-engined, highly-engineered tractor that is capable of producing 6,000 hp.

2

MONSTER TRUCKS

Bigfoot – the original III

IF YOU LOOK AT A SUCCESSFUL company closely you will find out many times that the entire operation started as a hobby or grew from a personal necessity of the owners, rather than a finely executed plan of action meant to climax at a certain point and time. In many ways, this describes the Chandler's Bigfoot operation. According to Bob Chandler it all started as a need to service his own Ford 4x4 truck.

Being one to share his talents for fixing trucks, Bob soon began fixing problems for friends from his home driveway. Like most of us just starting a new job, he did this on a part-time basis along with his full-time job of carpentry. Well, what started as a service-oriented idea soon overwhelmed their friends, assistants and their neighbours. In 1975 it was time to get serious about a storefront business.

It wasn't long after that first breath of life for Midwest Four Wheel Drive that the first of their Bigfeet (that's what you call several Bigfoots, isn't it?) came into existence. Like all trucks they've owned, all of them have been Ford and painted the official Ford dark blue colors. The exception is the new Ranger and Aerostar van.

Since the days of the driveway auto repairs and the help by parents and friends, the

▲

Outfitted with newly installed 2½-ton Rockwell military axles, four 18.4 x 16.1 tyres per axle and the 460 cid Ford engine, this was the first of many charity events that Bigfoot was to raise money for.

◄

Little did the world–or Bob Chandler–know this mild '74 F-250 outfitted with white spoke rims, 12 x 16.5 Delta tyres and the first of the steerable axles would turn into the business it is today.

►

By 1981 the Midwest logo had disappeared from the doors as seen from this shot from the movie, Take This Job and Shove It. Bob actually drove many of the scenes himself due to the beating the stuntmen were giving the truck. Even Bob did some damage to the windscreen of Bigfoot II in this last scene of the movie. Damage during filming of the movie included eight blown shock absorbers, a bent frame and two bent wheels.

Chandler operation has grown to be the one symbol in the four-wheel drive world that is synomonous with the fat-tired, car crushing trucks that have become known as 'monster trucks'. The total operation known today as Bigfoot 4x4, Inc. and Midwest Four Wheel Drive & Performance Center is housed on three acres of land, uses 25,000 square feet of space for warehouses, sales and offices and employs roughly 50 men and women. To this day, Bob is still somewhat stunned as to the size of the operation, for when asked the obvious question about his aspirations in the earlier days, he thinks, adjusts his ever-present cowboy hat a little and tells you that he was always building the best performing truck he could. He admits to having some long-range plans, but as for now, 'We really don't know, we have so many things going on right now, we're playing it by ear'. Of course, even Bob has his secrets!

Bigfoot Beginnings

Although *Bigfoot* is without a doubt the most recognizable Ford truck ever conceived, Bob doesn't lay claim to being the first to use the military axles. Longtime friend and neighbour, Don DeGrasso had $2\frac{1}{2}$-ton axles under his *Beast* before Bob did. *Bigfoot,* however, was the first of what is now known as the monster truck!

According to Chandler, *Bigfoot* actually came about as a promotional gimmick and to meet the need to be able to get further afield. As they had opened the store in 1975, they had purchased a new '74 Ford with 360 CID engine and 4-speed gearbox to take the place of the tiring '67. 'I wanted products on my truck that I sold in the store and vice-versa, as a sales gimmick. I went to every kind of race I could find.' The first large tires used were Delta 12.00 x 16.5 on white spoke steel rims that Bob had a chance to use while returning from vacation in Alaska–the last lengthy vacation the Chandler family was to take!

The name *Bigfoot* actually came about as part of the racing that Bob and crew started with the '74. 'Every month we'd be changing things, adding products we sold. We'd race it, and keep breaking it, so we'd go to a bigger axle. When you get a bigger axle and everything works well for a while then you go to a bigger tire and then a bigger engine. It's a continuous battle; we're still changing parts the same way.'

Accordingly, the larger 460 CID Ford engine gave its share of problems. It seems that due to the new-found power, Bob was prone to putting his foot too far into the throttle, consequently breaking parts. The coining of the truck's name was purely coincidental as a reference to Bob's big feet.

By the late 70s *Bigfoot* had become an entity unto itself. In fact, the interest in such vehicles was growing to such a point that *Bigfoot* was featured on the cover and several pages inside of Petersen's *4-Wheel & Off-Road* magazine, the leading off-road publication in those days. It was soon after the media coverage started that the off-road performance industry started taking notice of the public's appreciation of

Bigfoot and other similar trucks as the tall street-driven truck craze started its short-lived years.

Of the stunts that have been standard for monster trucks, the car crush has concerned Bob and Marilyn the most as they perceived it as bad for the image they wanted for their company and products. As *Bigfoot* grew so has their interaction with many children's and civic groups around their town and state. Hence, the worry over their appearance.

According to Bob, due to the destructive nature of car-crushing, they labored for several months before their first public performance of such a stunt. 'First time we were asked to do that, Jim Kramer–my number one man–and I went out to a field and videotaped it just for showing in the shop. A promotor saw it and wanted us to do it in front of a crowd. We kept telling him no. Now, no matter what else we do, people want to see a car crush, that's number one. I don't know why, but it is entertainment I guess.'

By the dawn of the 80s the monster truck had become an accepted part of the off-road scene. By this time several other truck names were making their presence known to both the public and media. It wasn't long before *Bigfoot* had its first major movie role in *Take This Job and Shove It,* and went on to star in other movies, TV, video and commercials, *Cannonball Run II* and *Police Academy II* being the most widely seen.

As *Bigfoot* was such a giant success, there came those that were both innovators and imitators. By 1982 there were at least a half-dozen trucks similar to it, equipped with like tires and axles and of similar appearance. Names like *USA-1, Bear Foot* and *King Kong* were to the legions of offroad fans what the Aston Martin was to

You can always tell where Bigfoot's *10 foot-tall tires* have been–they leave behind a clear trail! Bob found eight of these tires in Seattle, Washington in 1984. They were originally designed for vehicles traversing the snow. They make the truck over 14-feet wide.

James Bond movies. With the competition growing ever closer, Bob knew he had better have another card up his sleeve! However, the "birth" of *Bigfoot II* had innovations unlike *Bigfoot I.* Complete with 5-ton Rockwell military axles, 66-inch Goodyear Terra tires, gear steering capabilities and supercharged engine, the future of these trucks was showcased in one vehicle. In the years 1982 thru 1985 it seems that the national off-road magazines were debuting a new truck almost every month. Not all of them were unusual or creative either; most were created as a commercial venture patterned after the leading names.

With the introduction of *Bigfoot's* III, IV and V as well as the mid-size Ford Ranger and the Ford Aerostar van, it's no doubt that Bigfoot 4x4 Inc. is the clear leader in this unique motorsport industry as only several other teams either have or are planning more than one truck in the near future. The *Bigfoot* crews are not concerned with that illusionary position of being number one in too many aspects, as that position is somewhat akin to the days of the western gunslinger–there's always a new kid in town waiting to shoot you down! However, with a fan club that numbers in the tens of thousands, it's going to be hard to knock Bob Chandler's *Bigfoot* from the hard-earned throne it sits upon. But then take most any weekend around the nation and you'll be able to watch him defend his throne yet one more time.

As in any form of competition, change is the only constant that can be counted on, for it is change that keeps the fellows in second place in that position. With six Bigfoot F-250 longbed trucks, a mid-sized Ranger and an Aerostar van all lodged at the shop, the face of any Bigfoot can be changed at almost any appearance. This can be very confusing to even the most ardent admirer. Therefore, to give you a clue as to the scope of this team we present the following statistics of the Bigfoot team.

Bigfoot I
1974 Ford F-250 pickup
Engine: 640 cid aluminum Alan Root Ford V-8 Supercharged by a Blower Drive Service 8-71 GMC blower with 3 custom Predator carburetors.
Transmission: Ford C-6 automatic with $2^1/2$ ton transfer case that connects to 5-ton Rockwell military axles, Henry's custom-made hardened axles, Detroit Lockers and Warn lockout hubs.
Wheels: 66x43x25 Goodyear Terra tires with aluminum wheels.

This, the original *Bigfoot* is primarily used for hill-climbs and running the mud. Due to its high wheel speeds, tremendous horsepower (approximately 1,100 hp) and low weight (10,500lb) it has excellent weight to power compared to the other trucks in their stable.

For the greatest part, all six Bigfoots run approximately the same running gear (for instance the same transmission and 5-ton axles). Bob tells us that this allows interchanging of parts if necessary. The obvious differences are items like the base engines, for instance; *Bigfoot II* uses a Ford Motorsport 460CID engine with two Predator carburetors and a 6-71 BDS blower, *Bigfoot* III uses the 429 cid Ford engine bored to 460 cid and the same intake systems.

The big difference in engines come into play with *Bigfoot V,* the truck with the ten-foot tall tundra tires. This '74 Ford is the heaviest of all the trucks with a gross weight of almost 19,000lb. It's sole usage is the crushing of cars and the occasional mud run. Due to the use of the planetary style of hubs and the reduction of gear multiplication they effect on the truck, this truck uses the lowest power engine in the fleet, a 429 cid Ford V-8 with one Predator carburetor. It doesn't have any use for horsepower, just the low gearing.

The suspension is very similar for all of the six longbed trucks as they use Monroe custom-made shocks and suspension fabricated by the crew of Midwest Four Wheel Drive. The amount of shocks vary from 12 to 18 per truck, depending upon the application of the truck. *Bigfoot IV* uses 18 shocks due to its 15,000lb weight and racing usage, whereas *Bigfoot I* uses 14 shocks with its lesser weight.

Ms. Bigfoot is an entirely different truck, as due to its short wheelbase and light weight, it has a propensity for standing on its rear bumper. Even though it has the second most powerful engine (an Alan Root aluminum 571 cid V-8 with BDS 8-71 blower and twin Predators) in the fleet, the truck uses just 48-inch tall tires. The suspension is an air bag, five link, multi-shock arrangement built by the shop. With exception of the Aerostar van, it's the lightest truck in the fleet.

All of the vehicles have in common their Ford Motor Company origin, the same sponsors, air boost brakes (all drum except for *Bigfoot IV*), hydraulic rear steering and use 66 inch tall Goodyear Terra tires. The ranger and Aerostar use 48-inch tall tires as 66-inch tires look ungainly.

The one thing all of Chandler's trucks have in common is that they're always detailed, well presented and have yet to miss even one of their show bookings in all these ten years of showmanship. How many of us can say we've never missed a day of work in ten years?

▲

Even at its 10,500 lb weight, Bigfoot I is still used primarily for mud bogs and hill climbs due to its 640cid engine that helps make tremendous wheel speeds possible.

▲

However, even the mighty Bigfoot has never made it through the Jamboree mud bog.

25

▲
Every one of the Bigfoot's use Ford V-8s, BDS blowers, Predator racing carburetors, Hedman headers and feature a tilting hood. According to Bob, it's not just horsepower that monsters require, it's carefully contrived gearing.

▼
As shown in this photo, Bigfoot V is equipped with eight tyres that help it attain a 30,000 lb weight, a 22-ft width and almost 16 feet of height. Top speed is about 40 mph.

Above:

With the new aerodynamic bodystyles being introduced in Spring 1987, Bigfoot and several others will be sporting updated sheetmetal. This will make it even harder to know which foot the number is on.

Top:

Keeping the trucks moving are several Ford motorhomes, a tractor-trailer rig and open-bed trailers. This allows security and a 'home on wheels' feeling for the several crews that keep the company's trucks on the road.

At the Oakland Coliseum in October 1986 Jim Kramer had Bigfoot IV airborn enough to clear three-and-half out of six cars. It looks great to us, but from Jim's standpoint he has to be very careful to avoid door posts and be prepared for the second landing. Like he said, 'A 10,000 lb truck weighs 30,000 lb when it lands, if you hit the gas pedal something has to break?!

The last truck over the cars in these 'monster races' is usually the luckiest, as they're easier to approach and easier to land on. The more cars, the safer it is to land, as then the possibility of being straddled over two cars is lessened. At the end of the show, the cars are removed by forklifts.

Ms Bigfoot features a 'baby blue' paint scheme, that sets it apart from its larger brothers. It also has a 112-inch wheelbase with 48-inch Goodyear Terra tyres, and is a whole bunch of fun to drive according to the prime driver, grandmother Janice Oliver.

Weighing over 2,000 lb apiece, those 10 ft tyres are a job for several men and a crane when they're loaded onto their trailer for the ride back to base. Bob Chandler gets the easy job of operating the crane!

Before Bigfoot V can unload its tyres, it has to wash between its toes.

IV
The
Innovators

IT WASN'T LONG AFTER *BIGFOOT'S* FIRST large public appearance in Las Vegas, Nevada in 1977, that the big truck fad started to roll along like a small freight train–one that was to gain a full head of steam by the end of the decade. Meanwhile, another Ford truck was making quite a name for itself around its home state area. Named *King Kong,* the ideas were already forming for *Bigfoot vs King Kong* battles. Two legendary creatures, Bigfoot (or Sasquatch as the American Indian named him), vs the Hollywood movie imagination. What a matchup!

By 1982 the monster truck craze had planted its huge Goodyear Terra tires firmly upon the front of magazine covers, TV interview shows, children's shows and had even been offered starring roles in major movies. Of course, for those wise enough (and wealthy enough) to see what was happening, the opportunities to get into this new entertainment were at their maximum at this stage of the show.

As *King Kong* and owner, Jeff Dane, were making their names in Texas (if you ask any Texan, where else would you find a big truck?), so were newcomers Fred Shafer, Jack Wilman, Everett Jasmer, Don DeGrasso (*Bigfoot's* neighbour) and the Spiker brothers, David and Steve. These were the names that made themselves known in the first few years of the 1980s with names such as; *Bear Foot, Taurus, USA-1, D-Beast, Spiker's All American* and *Spiker's Eagle.*

It didn't take more than a few months for what could be called imitations to follow on the heels of these innovators of monster truckdom. In fact, by 1983 there were even toy monster trucks, miniature ride-along *Bigfoot's* by Playskool and other novelties. Whatever the brand of allegiance of American-built truck; Ford, Chevy, GMC or Dodge, they were all there.

It wasn't until the years 1982-1984 that the first 'small monster' arrived as Bear Foot's Chevy S-10, Ed Socie's Creative *Evolution Datsun,* Mark Dye's *Fly-N-Hi Toyota* and Bigfoot's *Ms Bigfoot,* a Ford Ranger.

Monster Showmanship

Like any entertainment, the acts have to evolve from time to time, otherwise the paying audiences will no longer show up for the circus that these machines perform in. It soon became apparent that diving into mud pits, pulling the sled and simply 'walking' over junk cars was as everyday as sunrise and sunset.

According to *Bear Foot's* owner, Fred Shafer, he pulled a wheelstand 'by accident' while in performance one day. He sat the truck up high, the crowd loved it, and ever since then the wheelstand has been one of *Bear Foot's* favorite stunts. Of course, it didn't take too much time for the others to follow suit and put their stamp on this stunt. Even Fred admits that with his short wheelbase S-10 it can be tricky if the cars to be crushed are approached incorrectly with too much power. This can result in a complete rollover backwards, something *Bear Foot* has done once. Fortunately, due to roll cages and helmets there are rarely any injuries, even when 15,000lb falls on top of the driver.

As showmanship is really what these footrucks are all about, there had to be unusual things done with them–publicity stunts, as they could be called. Due to his ownership of a game farm, *Bear Foot's* Fred Shafer used twin American Black Bear cubs as the tie-in with his truck's name. He even once chained the truck to a stadium floor where he 'smoked' all four 73-inch, 1,000lb Goodyear tires for a show. According to Fred, 'it peeled the topping off the concrete which the promoter had to pay for 'cause it wrinkled the slick surface on the floor'. However, *Bear Foot's* claim to fame was crushing large passenger buses. This performance is now carried out by Jack Wilman's monster truck, *Taurus.*

Like many of these truck builders, Everett Jasmer has more than just an off-road truck interest. He owns Off Road Specialties, a 4x4 retail performance shop, of which he makes full use with almost complete in-house fabrication of *USA-1*. With a name like *USA-1,* it's obviously a Chevy!

As others were building trucks using standard power of exotic, supercharged, nitrous-injected V8s, Jeff Dane was fitting the first twin-turbo diesel into a monster truck. Not content to rest upon that idea, he has lately built what is clearly the most overpowered truck. From real stump-pulling diesel torque to clear overkill of cubic inches, *Awesome Kong* is quite an engineering marvel to see. Not content with having this one truck, Dane has lately built an all-out racing truck of 10,500lb that's used just for the monster races that feature obstacle courses.

One of the larger names on the scene was at that time the Spiker family. Two Fords strong, their presence was national at one time. One of their biggest claims to fame was at the 1984 Off-Road Jamboree where they presented their Sister, Bonnie, and her Chevy S-10. This was before the Chandler's were ready to debut their '85 Ranger.

By the opening of the year 1985, the monster truck scene was heading for epidemic proportions. Crossings of famous lakes and rivers, crushing cars and buses–even those cars that had some smoke bombs and fire emanating from them–and wheelstands before simple car crushes, were becoming mundane. The second stage rocket of the monster scene was about to ignite!

USA-1
Owner: Everett Jasmer
Truck type: 1970 Chevy longbed
Engine: aluminium block 540 cid Chevrolet
Intake system: Two Predator carburetors and BDS 6-71 GMC Supercharger. NOS nitrous system
Transmission/transfer case: Turbo 400 automatic with 223 Rockwell
Axles: 5-ton military Rockwell with 10.26 final ratio
Differentials: Detroit Lockers with Warn hubs
Wheels/tires: custom-made 25x36 inch aluminum with 66/43 x 25 inch Goodyear Terra tires
Shocks: 16
Height: under 12ft
Weight: 12,000lbs

Bear Foot I, and Lil 'Bear Foot
Owner: Fred Shafer
Truck type: '86 Chevy, and '82 S-10
Engine: 505 cid Chevy S-10–454 cid Chevy
Intake system: BDS 8-71 blower with Enderle F.I. S-10-two Holley 660cfm carburetors, BDS 6-71 blower. Nitrous
Transmission/transfer case: TH 400 automatic, 5-ton military case S-10 ½-ton case
Axles: 5-ton military (both) S-10 5-ton with Corvette differentials used above them

In 1983, Everett Jasmer debuted USA-1's all-new bodystyle with updated graphics from Dan Patterson. According to Everett, the name came while mowing his lawns one day. 'It's got a unique sound, a patriotic tie to it, a Chevrolet tie to it, and I wanted to be the number 1 Chevrolet'. It took many hours to tie the body and a framework together so that the flip-up 'flopper' body was rigid. Scheel bucket seats, Deist automatic fire-extinguishing system and hydraulics are all inside cab.

Like all the trucks, USA-1 uses a V-8 'big block' engine that uses a GMC supercharger (blower), dual (Predator) carburetors and nitrous oxide. Approximate horsepower is eight hundred.

▲

With the 66-inch Goodyear tyres inflated with 20+ psi of air, USA-1 set a world monster truck record on Saturday, October 13th, 1984 by 'paddling' some 3 miles in the mighty Mississippi River. Some other trucks have also done water shows, several having ended with the truck upside-down when the tires deflated or the truck capsized.

Charging into the mud, with a wall of mud in front of those 4-foot wide Terra tyres, Everett and USA-1 have yet to vanquish the Jamboree mud which usually halts monster trucks with fiery results. The damage here was very minor, but this time USA-1 finished a few feet ahead of Bigfoot.

◄

Despite the tall tyres, the lack of a running start is able to halt Bigfoot's charge.

One secret behind crushing cars safely is approaching them correctly. You want to put the rear tyres at the doors of the first car, making sure you land on the second car hoping that the tires grip so that you don't slide off the truck. The problem here, was that the third 'victim' was a mid-sized car that was a few feet too short on length for the passenger-side tyre to get its best grip.

►

Continued from page 33

Wheels/tires: 74-inch Goodyear. S10; 66 or
74-inch Goodyear
Shocks: 16 S-10–16
Height: 14 ft. S-10–11 ft plus
Weight: 16,000 lbs S-10–12,000 lbs

Awesome Kong
Owner: Jeff Dane
Truck: '85 Ford
Engine: Allison V-12, 1,710 cid
Intake System: 4 Predator carburetors
Transmission/transfer case: CLT-750 Allison
automatic w/drop box. Weight 1,800 lbs
Differentials/Axles: 70-ton rated Eaton,
Rockwell and many handmade parts.
Equipped with 90-degree gear drive,
selectable from cab.
Wheels/tires: Handmade steel 32x38-inches,
74-inch Goodyear Super Terra Grip.
Shocks: 28 Freon-assisted gas shocks
Height: 11 ft. 6 ins.
Weight: 21,500 lbs

Facing page:
However, for USA-1 *the victory has its
penalties. Mud and water play havoc on seals
and gaskets in the running gear that's been
trudging through this mire.*

▶

For Bigfoot, *win or lose,
there's an hour of
getting those tall tyres
hosed-off.*

Spiker's Eagle
Owner: Steve Spiker
Truck type: '84 F-250 Ford
Engine: 488 cid Chevrolet
Intake System: 2 Holley 750cfm carburetors,
tunnel ram and nitrous oxide system
Transmission/transfer case: Allison AT 540,
2-speed gear reduction gearbox and
$2^1/2$-ton military transfer case
Axles: 5-ton military Rockwell.
Wheels/tires: 36 x 32 chrome modular
wheels and 73-inch Goodyear Super Terra
Grip tires
Shocks: 16 Monroe Magnum 70's
Height: 12 ft. plus
Weight: 15,000 lbs

Spiker's All American

Owner: David Spiker
Truck type: '83 F-250 Ford
Engine: 488 cid Chevrolet
Intake system: 2 Holley carburetors, tunnel ram and 2 300 hp nitrous oxide systems
Transmission/transfer case: Allison 4-speed automatic AT 540 and 2$\frac{1}{2}$-ton Timken transfer case.

Axles: 5-ton Rockwell military
Wheels/tires: 32 x 38-inch chrome steel and 73-inch Goodyear Super Terra Grip tires
Shocks: 16 Monroe 70-series
Height: 12 ft. plus
Weight: 14,000 lbs

▲

Little Bear Foot *(an S-10 Blazer) was the first of the few mid-sized monsters. It's unique in that the driveshaft connects to a Corvette differential which then connects to the Rockwell 5-ton axles. This drive system was necessary to lessen the driveshaft pinion entry angle that was detrimental to U-joint and pinion life.*

◀

Since it's only 3-feet tall, the 'baby bear' is used for running around the stadium rather than car crushing. The short wheelbase allows very quick wheelstands at speeds over 30 mph.

At the Anaheim, *California show recently*, Bear Foot's *quick steering and high roll center gave way to the forces of gravity. Due to the well-built in-cab steel cage and helmet, Fred walked away with bruises only. The damage to the body was estimated at $10,000, so Fred will acquire the new Chevy '87 sheetmetal instead of repairing this damage.*

Getting a monster truck into the air is not accomplished with the greatest of ease nor comfort. As Fred approaches the five 'victims' at about 25 mph, the front end lifts over the first car to launch itself skyward. At which point he takes his foot off the gas pedal . . .

▼

. . .floats over the first three cars, and lands squarely on the roof of the fourth.

One of Little Bear Foot's *favorite shows is with its four 66-inch 'paws'. As you can see, it's easy to track a bear when its pawprints are this large. Notice the angle of the differential input.*

The tilt hood makes for custom touch as does chrome on 454 cid Chevy engine. Artwork is also real nice touch.

Key to pages 42 & 43

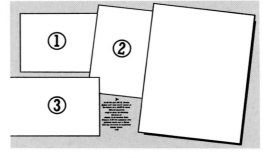

①

As Awesome Kong *weighs in at approximately 20,000 lb, it's the heaviest monster truck around. Notice the hubs are much larger than on other trucks shown.*

②

Back in the mid-70s Jeff started with King Kong, *his first Ford. Powered by a diesel engine and running gear, he soon decided that he wanted the 'ultimate engine' his company could fit into a pickup bed. This V-12 Allison fills the bed with a horrendous sound from twenty-four exhaust stacks that remind you of WW II. The bed lifts with hydraulics for easy service, and allows fans to gaze at the huge engine. Imagine if this engine was using fuel injection and a supercharger. Maybe it could climb the Empire State Building?*

③

Engineering is the middle name of Awesome Kong, *the second in Jeff Dane's monster lineage. The bodystyle is a stepside Ford that had its bed filled to the brim with 1,710 cubic inches of V-12 Allison aircraft engine, that is capable of producing over 2,000 hp in full-race trim. Look closely, and you'll find the door handles were lowered for easier entry.*

At 5ft 2in and 105 lb, Bonnie Spiker isn't what you'd expect as the driver of a 10,000 lb truck. Like all monsters, entry is done by climbing the tyres as shown. In its finished form, Bonnie's S-10 was equipped with gullwing doors and a flip-up bed that revealed its reinforced factory frame.

If you like old-iron, you can't beat Don DeGrasso's military-style Dodge Power Wagon, D-Beast. Although Don was one of the very first with military axles, and then tall tires, he hasn't made the public impression as he likes to use it in off-roading fun. This unfortunately has taken its toll on the truck twice now, and has resulted in some minor injuries to Don, too. The murals on each door are some of the best artwork on any truck. The interior is just as neat.

Facing page, top:
It may look great to spectators, but immersing these trucks in water ruins all the seals, and takes several days of work to re-lubricate the drive train, at quite an expense. What price publicity?

Not many owners engineer both hood and bed hydraulic systems, as it uses yards of wiring and a large battery system. The Spiker's original Ford was the first of three monsters in a family that owns eleven 4x4 trucks total. Like all the original trucks, drum brakes and a reinforced factory frame are used.

45

V Creative Evolution

LIKE IMITATORS OF FASHION CLOTHING of a great designer, those who have followed into this 'circus' in the last few years have their own interpretation of the original designs. Some call it copying, some call it flattery and in some cases, it's even been called theft. Whatever the term, it's clear that most of the newcomers in this game are motivated by a desire for something other than getting rich quickly. For some it's the competitive spirit within them, the drive to succeed in the goals they've set in life. For many I've spoken to, it's the opportunity of travelling across the USA and Canada, the freedom of the road and the chance for adventure that comes about while in transit from show to show, zig-zagging across the continent.

Of course, for some, the financial rewards can be great. However, for most, the legendary pot of gold at the end of the rainbow never quite appears, for travel costs and the upkeep of the one truck can take large chunks of money.

Each one of the new vehicles–they're no longer just trucks–is searching for its own identity within the ever-growing field. An image is usually created by giving the vehicle an interesting name that for some reason seems reminiscent of a mythical creature, motion picture figure or something destructive in nature. One of the older truck owners says he wonders when the imagination or supply of names will run out?

For the most part, these newcomers will have to learn many times faster than their veteran counterparts due to such phenomenons as the 'Battle of the Monster Trucks' as their acts are now called. Their differences will have to be great and the performances worthy of encores from the crowds. Little innovations like aircraft steering 'joysticks', flip-top 'flopper' bodystyles, 'clamshell' style doors that hinge at the top of the cab instead of the factory placement, flames belching from the chrome headers peering from the hood line and immaculately prepared undercarriages with varying colors and chromes are just part of what is starting to take place.

By combining the sounds and sights of the drag racing vehicle with top-notch, show-quality attention to details, the monster truck of the coming years will garner greater attention that those entrants that are sedately dressed in black undercarriage paint and a mild body color. After all, that is what showmanship is all about!

One of the most interesting stories about building a monster truck came when I met Don Maples of Huntsville, Alabama. Although he had the occasional help of friends, many long nights and cold mornings before sunrise were spent cutting cardboard templates and lifting a large industrial grinder, that eventually would put Don in the hospital with back injuries. Working in a garage out back of his family's house that measured 40x24x10-ft high, Don managed to put together what was one of the first larger than factory frames for a monster truck.

Back in 1983, Gael and Carol Morgan built this 1981 Ford Bronco XLT for some off-roading fun for the family. As Gael puts it, he was tired of getting stuck in the winter storm's mud. Using 48 inches of Goodyear tire, $2^1/_2$-ton military axles, and a BDS-blown 427 cid engine, it's a 7,000 lb, $8^1/_2$ ft fun Ford.

Key to previous pages

Here you can see how Don used the stock frame over some boxed steel as it allows greater strength and also several inches of height without using flimsy body lifts. The engine is a blown, dual-carburated 513 cid Chevy of about 700 hp. Like most 4-wheelers, Don uses a winch and a custom bumper for dress. These are a Warn 12,000 lb unit and Reflexion custom. Although Don did some of the paint, Ronnie Farmer did the murals and truck body. It's clean enough to enter in a car show!

If there is one standout of engineering ability in the monster truck field, it's the Fly-N-Hi Toyota. Building some of the nicest trucks in the nation, Mark and Mike Dye built this beauty at their company's Phoenix, Arizona shop some three years ago, and have as yet to be upstaged by anyone. The front end of this Toyota features 66x43-inch tyres with custom wheels, 5-ton military axles with hydraulic steering, the first use of the GM disc brake on military axles, hand-made shock brackets and is finished in cadmium and chrome plating and electro-powder plating.

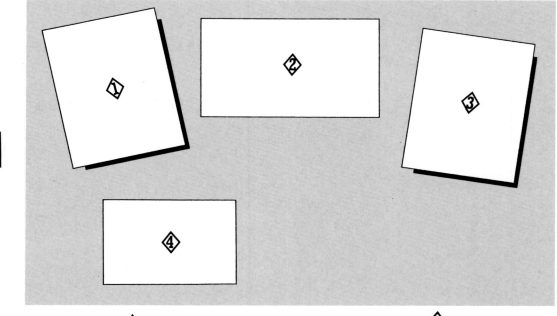

Standing just over 12 ft, Brett Engelman's Michigan Ice Monster weighs 13,000 lb and uses the usual military running gear. The etched glasswork is unique.

Unlike most monster trucks, Fly-N-Hi doesn't have the asset of rear steering. One reason is the size of the small body that would have clearance problems with tyres.

Two of the loudest and most aggressive monsters, are the creations of Kirk and Kevin Dabney of Fayettville, North Carolina. Kirk's Thunder Beast, a '68 Chevy Camaro, has undergone building twice as it started out as a monster with smaller axles and drivetrain. The special features of the Camaro are; hydraulic steering via a helicopter 'joystick' control, airbag suspension with thirty shocks, 20-ton Clark planetaries and 2-speed air-shifted gearbox.

A

One of the best engine bays in any truck, this one sports a supercharged, dual carbureted 350 cid Chevy and several months of handiwork on the frame rails, as they've all been sanded and filled. If it's not painted, it's chromed or plated.

B

Jake Henke's immaculately detailed '72 Chevy El Camino is a show truck turned monster wheelstander and car crusher. Named Aces High, *this truck can stand on its hind quarters at will, due to the weight transfer box located under the bed (the small wheels are barely visible).*

D & E

Mustang enthusiasts must cringe when they see Tommy Bryant's '67 fastback Mustang! Classic 'stang now features 460 cid Ford engine, 15-ton Rockwell planetary axles and unique parallel-drive system that eliminates U-joint breakage.

Pony Express *is but one of many new monsters that is using a complete steel box-frame to support a body. Undercarriage is mostly military.*

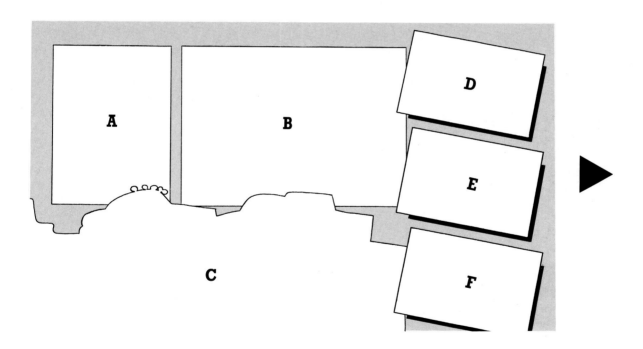

C

Hawaiian Punch *and* Terminator *hail from Southern California. Both use standard military drive train and compete in monster races.*

F

Black Knight Chevy *uses flip-up body, clamshell doors and the usual military running gear. Owned by Mike Brady of the NMBA, the truck sees lots of mud bogs.*

Of the new monster trucks, Seth Doulton's Skoal Bandits and Copenhagen Crusher are amongst the front runners. A businessman, Seth built the first truck (Skoal Bandits) using his business knowledge and a rare, beautiful '58 Chevy Cameo pickup. Not only did he use a rare truck, but he also powered it with a V-12 Jaguar engine that was built to put out a solid 600 hp to the usual military drive train of these trucks.

Used not only as a car crusher, the Copenhagen Crusher *is also outfitted with many comforts of a street-driven truck: Blaupunkt 600 watt stereo with remote control, custom seats, automatic transmission and hydraulic hood and bed are amongst the unusual options.*

Not only is the Skoal Bandit *powered by the most unusual engine, a V-12 Jaguar with muitiple Weber carburetors, it's also the most valuable. There are not that many '58 Chevy Cameos around these days.*

Long wheelbase trucks are much easier to drive and control over cars. Mike Welch's Peterbilt-bodied creation is but one of several he has debuted over the last year. It's power is a small cid Chevy, located behind the cab.

SUPER PETE

MIKE WELCH

▲

This Bronco makes a very unusual monster as it's short wheelbase can make for a wild ride when it sets up on its hind quarters. Many of the southern trucks run the Confederate flag for show.

◄

More a fun 4x4 than monster, Ringo's Revenge uses 1¹/₂-ton military axles and small flotation tyres for its 8 ft height.

59

Starting with a '78 Ford Bronco, Brian Shell built his own frame, covered 250 pieces with chrome, lowered the door handles, added the standard military drive train and covered everything with 11-gallons of Imron paint . . .

. . . as can be seen from the undercarriage of his Showtime Ford.

Interesting Toyota uses 5-ton military hardware and airbag/shock absorber suspension to handle car crushing. Seeing as it's a Toy-ota, the key provides windup power!

Due to the short wheelbase of the Jeep, the use of a 'wheelie bar' is mandatory to stop rollovers. Name came from paint scheme of Corvette red colors by Jim Craw.

▲

The 'Battle of the Monster Trucks' show usually starts with a sled pull. Notice the front-end lift on Samson I, as he pulls some 40,000 lb one-hundred feet. 5-54

After they were released from the tow hitch, Pony Express and Samson I set about crushing a set of cars. Most races are done with two sets of six cars, the last set being crushed after a U-turn at the top of the track.

▼

It's not always the first truck on the cars that wins the race. Axle breakage, slipping off the cars due to too quick a steering input, and several other factors make or break the competitors.

Bob Holman and family were involved in the car show scene when they decided to transform their '73 Chevy into a monster truck. A family and business affair, Bob has even driven this beauty into the mud pits. Possibly the most detailed monster truck, it features lots more than these two photos portray.

Facing page, far left:
Kevin Presnell owns two trucks, Gentle Ben I & II, a Chevy and Ford. As he owns two black bear cubs and a 4x4 store, he figured the bear tie-in was a natural.

Facing page, top right:
Built from 40s firetruck, we're not sure if Mike Welch's vehicle is a mud truck or car crusher?

▲

In the spirit of the car customizers of old, Jeff Bainter of Yakima, Washington has taken a '86 Jeep CJ-7 and widened the body by 15-inches and lengthened it by 12-inches to produce Hot Stuff *the first really custom monster truck. Only on the stage since late 1986, Jeff and his crew have become one of the new sensations in the sport.*

One of the problems of using the smaller and prone-to-breakage 2$\frac{1}{2}$-ton Rockwell axles, is shown in these two photos of Leadfoot, *a Chevy El camino. As he reached the third car, the axle hub gave way . . .*

. . . and the tire rolled to the sidelines.

**VI
Here's
mud in your eye**

AT ONE TIME IN OUR LIVES, WE'VE ALL played in the mud or traversed that ominous puddle of muck that looks like it might swallow us up in one gulp. That's what the mud bogs and mud drags are all about; to conquer the ominous black pit of specially-built muck.

Although there are monster trucks that do run the mud, for the greater part, 'mud runners' are purposely-built vehicles with a single intent. Speed and traction are words to live and die by in this sport, for it's those vehicles that have both of these attributes that take home the small amounts of cash that are usually offered. Breaking the silence of the crowd's attention, these unique 2-wheel and 4-wheel drive vehicles can 'fly' across 200 feet of 4 foot deep quagmire in times as swift as 3 seconds for the buggie class, and a hair under 4 seconds for the monster truck class.

In these mud sports there are but two rules: time and distance. In the case of the extremely lightweight buggies, they had better hope their brakes are working well, as barriers of concrete and cars await them in stadium shows.

There are several classes of competitors arranged by how many driven axles there are (2-wheel or 4-wheel drive): whether they are factory stock or have a slightly modified engine, drive train and street-legal tires; and the final class of too many modifications to count with tractor tires and lots of horsepower. The classes are commonly referred to as Stock, Modified, Pro Stock, Super Pro or Experimental. It depends upon the organization sponsoring the event as to what the classes are called.

The monster trucks run the mud simply for exhibition purposes. That is, with the exception of those monster trucks built with huge tractor tires that are built for mud-running.

The big difference between the monster trucks that we've previously presented and monster mud runners is in their tires, weight, transfer case style, and engine and its location.

The tires are usually Rice and Cane style, the name taken from the fields they are used in. Measuring some 64 inches tall, the tread is obviously different and the tire width is far less, that is unless the truck is running four of these tires per axle for deep mud pits.

The weight is usually less, depending upon whether it's built purely for mud runs or partial duty as a car crusher. Eight thousand pounds and a height of nine to eleven feet at the top of the cab are standard for these monster mudders. As location of the weight is critical, the engine is usually moved rearward (into the cab) as much as several feet. This helps the front-to-back weight balance.

As they need light weight for speed, these large trucks use a chain-driven transfer case instead of the heavy and power-robbing military-style of other monster trucks. As the power is usually derived from single or dual carburetors and nitrous oxide, the power is a little lower in some cases. The axles however, are usually the $2^1/2$ ton or 5-ton Rockwell units necessary for strength.

The mud bogs/drags were around long before monster trucks. And they are gaining greater popularity as they are something everyone can get into for little or no money, depending upon the class they wish to compete in. It's simple, mucky fun for those with a competitive spirit.

According to Ken Donat, Events Director for the USHRA, it can take five days to set up an event, complete with mud pit and two pulling tracks. In the case of Oakland Stadium (shown here) it can take a day or two to clean up.

▼

Depending upon the size of the stadium and area required for a show, the entire floor or part of has to be covered with: 2,000 square yards of dirt; 1,600 4x8 foot plywood sheets; 60 rolls of 30x100 ft plastic; several hundred railroad ties; 10,000 gallons of water for the mud pits; and several tractors and crew.

▲
Cyclops *is one of the fastest monster mudders ever made. The time for 200-foot runs is consistently under 5-seconds. Even Gary Gardiner and* Cyclops *have met their match when it comes to the six feet of thick Jamboree mud.*

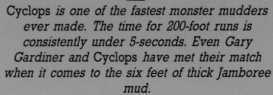

◀
Monster mudders are built similar to the normal car crushing trucks, except that they have little suspension, a lot less weight, an engine of less power, and 64-inch tyres that have very deep tread. Depending upon the pit, the dual tyres are optional.

Facing page, top:
Early sixties Ford Falcon uses tall mud tyres, large engine and 1-ton drive train to power it across the mud.

▲
Representative of what is normally driven in mudpits, this Ford is equipped with a 400-plus cubic inch engine and dual carburetors. Most wheels run standard Rice & Cane tires.

Facing page, top:
Psycho Chevy runs Super Pro class due to usage of large Rice & Cane tires. Notice fuel tank at front bumper.

Facing page, bottom:
At the drop of the flag, the tires grab for traction, mud flies rearwards and two Super Pro's hope they'll float across the mud. Unfortunately, one is bound to lose!

For 1987, Mike and Judy West are going to try their luck with this extremely potent 400-plus cid, blown, fuel injected dune buggy. Weighing in at about 1,500 lb, the problem will be keeping the front end from becoming airborne.

If you want to see some real mud bogging you have to watch for the Florida teams. Not only tops in Florida, Ron-Jon's trucks are also tops at the Jamboree each year. Believe it or not, it's a Corvette body. Notice how everything is sealed, the rack & pinion steering, 38-inch tall tires and enclosed cab.

▲

Built with a single seat, marine battery, oil coolers, radiator, drivers cage and small tires, Widow Maker *Chevy* competes in lower class than its brother Corvette.

▼

The inside of Mud Buster *is all business with center-mounted driver position, three gages, a glassfiber seat, harnesses and rollcage.*

75

▶ *Running in the modified class, this Toyota Landcruiser uses dual-wheels to aid in traction. Surprisingly enough, he made it through!*

▼ *During winter, this Ford's a snowplow, but at the fall Jamboree it makes exhibition runs in the obstacle course. It does very well!*

Held twice a year, the 4-Wheel & Off Road Jamboree brings together some of the best mudders from around the nation. The following shots are a sampling of that event.

This Ford T-bird always makes a great show. The tires resemble sand tires, but seem to have been regrooved.

▶ *Many of the mud runners appear to be based upon a Jeep body. Of course, they're all 4-wheel drive and have plenty of engine. In mud sports, if you're throwing mud you're moving. It isn't the same for truck and tractor pullers, as you'll soon see.*

◄◄

Most of the stadium mud bogs are just deep enough for the truck to disappear beneath the level of the photographer's camera or they get covered with a muddy disguise.

◄

Unfortunately, Mud Buster *didn't make it this time. The injection scoop is not real, just a look-alike.*

Bottom Centre:

Several of the fastest monster mudders use air bag suspension as it's lighter than steel springs and shocks. The differential is a GM 1-ton unit.

▼

Mud Lord *is possibly the fastest consistent monster mudder in the nation. At 7,000 lb Bernie Willis and truck can skip most mud in less than 4 seconds!*

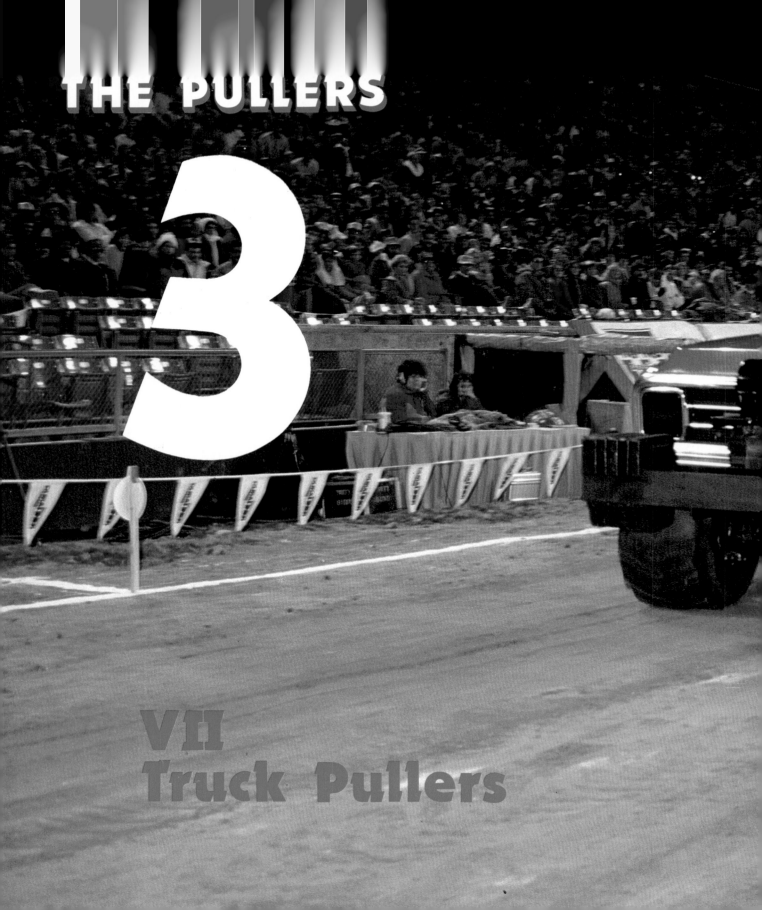

THE PULLERS

3

VII
Truck Pullers

SINCE THE DAYS OF THE PYRAMIDS, the building of Stonehenge and other unexplainable feats of engineering and strength, man has sought to pit the strength of his farming animals against the immovable or the insurmountable object. In modern days it was the horse, bred specifically for tug-of-wars between neighbours and friends on the weekends, and hauling the heaviest loads in the business days.

This type of contest hasn't really changed for hundreds of years. Today's 'horses' have names like; *Arias, Alan Root, Keith Black, Donovan, Ford Motorsport, Milodon* and *Rodeck.* All of them far more powerful and compact than even the wildest dreams of the first organized and recorded farm tractor pulls of the nineteen-twenties American midwest.

Today's tractor pulling has evolved into an international sport for all the family that has grown to encompass the truck racing and even facets of the drag racing sport. In essence, it's become the truly all-American motor sport that has spread its wings to entertain not only tens of millions of

Americans per year, but also the Australian and European people that have found this sport challenging and visually exciting. In fact, the NTPA rule book is now printed in several languages other than English.

Truck Pullers

Until the advent of the NTPA in 1969 and the growth of a standard rule book that ensued, the sport of pulling had little direction due to several regional clubs and associations writing rules that suited their own needs. Today, the NTPA has become the leading authority on the many facets of pulling and its international appeal. As pulling vehicles come in varying sizes, the NTPA has split them into six divisions and a total of sixteen weight classes. The truck classes are:

Four-Wheel Drive (FWD)–These trucks use a single V-8 engine augmented with fuel injection. No supercharging is allowed, so horsepower comes from high-octane fuels and knowledge of engine power characteristics. Running in the 5,800 and 6,200lb classes, the power is usually just under 1,000 hp. It's one of the most popular classes due to brand name loyalty in contests like Ford vs Chevy.

Two-Wheel Drive (TWD)–The newest class of puller, this class is taking the sport by storm. They compete at the same weight classes and have identical V-8 engines (with the addition of supercharging) to the FWD trucks. This is where the similarity ends, as they are similar in actions to the drag racing rail dragster when they leave the starting line. With the introduction of glassfiber bodies reminiscent of drag racing's 'funny cars', this division has become very popular with fans. Although these two classes are per NTPA rulings, they conform closely to those of other associations like the USHRA and others who sponsor truck pulling. Although truck pulling is the newest part of the pulling sport, it's by far the easiest to visualize and participate in for many spectators and competitors. As many of the competitors start by having a try at local pulls or county fairs, this part of the sport is something everyone can get into on a low-budget level.

However, low-budget should not be construed as inexpensive as just a single blown, injected 500cid V-8 will cost an average of $10,000, the aluminum rims and special tires up to $1,500 and then you have to purchase the special transmission and driveline components. The total could be as much as $20,000, depending upon the mechanical ability you possess. Then there's the hauling trailer and truck required to get everything to an event. As an old expression goes in the US: 'Speed costs money; how fast do you wanna go?'

The trucks raced are strictly US-built Dodge, Chevy, Ford and GMC brands, as this sport grew in the heartland of America. Imported trucks are not part of the makeup of this very staunch and patriotic sport. Just as the sponsors and products used in this sport are US companies and US-built products.

Built with one single purpose in mind, the aggressive truck owner seeking a regional or national title, and the accompanying money and titles will build but one truck. It's the spare engine parts (and whole engines) and drive trains that will cost them the most money, as the usual breakages are to minor engine components and axle shafts.

The one thing the four-wheel drive puller must possess is the ability to read the movement of the truck as it thunders down the track. Even though the truck has four-wheel drive, it's easy to succumb to the inevitable weight of the sled on the truck's hitch if they simply drive straight forward. Looking much like they are trying to avoid plastic road cones, most drivers move their front tires from side to side at the top of the track, as this allows the tyres greater grip when the truck is slowing down.

Unlike some of the classes in pulling, the two-wheel and four-wheel drive classes are pretty straightforward with less noise. Of course, the new two-wheel class has the excitement of the wheelstand that comes from having such a lightweight front and huge pulling tires out back. No doubt, this is also exciting for the driver at times! As the sport progresses, it seems that even the diehard tractor pullers are looking at this new class of NTPA pulling, and in some cases are building a truck in addition to their tractors. With the addition of the 'funny car' glassfiber body, the connection between the fans' everyday-driven automobile and the puller itself, should lead to more and more involvement by the major US auto manufacturers seeking exposure for new model cars. Just as they have done with that same class of racer in the NHRA for a decade or more. This undoubtedly will bring more and more of the big names into truck pulling as the cash sponsorship awards begin to outstrip those given for other classes.

On the other side of the fence, however, for shows that feature monster trucks, pullers and mudders, the truck puller in the two-wheel drive class is a firm part of the show with the first showing of the TWD truck class in late 1986. The two-wheel drive funny car bodies are usually for exhibition only, as there aren't many 'floppers' built at this time.

Seeing as the Longaker family is making their career with the US Army, this military pickup is a natural. It's also, naturally, fast, as this full pull shows.

A native of central California, Dan Coelho does nationwide truck pulling on the USHRA circuit. He also runs a KW truck named Jack Rabbit for exhibition runs.

Although hoods are not required, the exhaust tips must exit straight above. If you'll notice the placement of the front weights, you'll see they're centered as opposed to split between each side. Personal preference or good chassis distribution?

The guys that run both NTPA and USHRA circuits are easy to spot as they run large air filters like this Wildfire Ford.

Bob and Pam Bauman campaign Yellow Fever on the USHRA circuit. He does the wrenching and she does the driving. Study the frame closely and you'll notice there's no suspension at the rear and only coil springs and two shocks at the front. Yes, she does wear a fireproof suit and helmet.

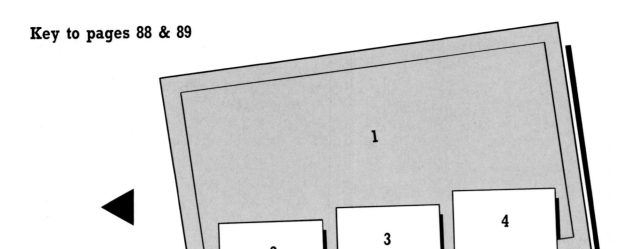

1

Being run in relatively stock sheetmetal,
Mother Goose *owner runs weights way out*
front, and hasn't carved-up body just in case
he decides to return to a street rod look.

2

As can be seen from this photo of Paula
Geuin's Black Gold *S-10, the truck must be*
kept within the white lines of the track.

3

It really doesn't matter what your puller looks
like, it's the power put to the ground that
matters. Brand and year of truck are not
known.

4

Initiated in late 1986, the USHRA now runs the
two-wheel drive class of pickup that was well
accepted by fans of the NTPA. Notice the
difference in tires over 4x4 class. The 4x4
class is allowed fuel injection, unlimited cubic
inches, but not supercharging. Notice
nose-down attitude.

One of the new two-wheel drive (TWD) class in the USHRA, Magnum Jr. sports a huge Ford engine with an 8-71 blower and a Hilborn fuel injector. Package is good for almost 1,500 hp.

▲

Nearing the 300-foot marker (just barely seen near front right tire), the tire speed slows but the traction increases due to greater bite with more tread on ground.

Many of the two-wheel drive classes use a flopper bodystyle due to access and crowd appeal. Notice that once the body is down in place, the driver is isolated from fuel and engine.

One thing common amongst top-rated truck pullers is their use of a Janke-built engine as the lettering indicates on Texas Bluebonnet. Notice drive train hoops and gearbox visible underneath truck.

A popular entry in the TWD class, is the new Ford Aerostar mini-van. At age 19, Darren Stephens has his hands full with this 1,700 hp, 588 cid puller.

Bottom left:
The red flag means that there is something going on at the hitch connection. The truck's transmission must remain in neutral until the green flag is given.

Old T-bucket runs Hilborn fuel injection, 400-plus cid Chevy and proves the old theory that the larger the engine, the greater the internal pressure that builds up. Valve cover cap came loose to cause this geyser blow.

The view most of the TWD drivers get for the first 50-feet or so. Wheelie bars prevent too high an attitude.

Representative of the long wheelbase trucks that seem to do well, these two (photos lower left and below) appeared at a pull at San Luis Obispo State College back in 1983.

VIII
Tractor Pullers

IF JUST A SINGLE ENGINE OF SOME 500 plus cubic inches is powerful, then several of these mastadons must be the force that can move mountains!

Moving the 'immovable' is what the tractor puller is all about, as even with the lowest weight modified tractor, the double or triple injected and/or supercharged aluminum engines can produce ear-splitting, ground-pounding ratings of approximately 1,500hp. The raw awesome force of several V-8 engines or triple V-12 aircraft engines attaining almost 9,000 hp is guaranteed to make one's knees quiver as it passes by.

Although the basic farm tractor was the very beginning of this sport, it's only seen at NTPA functions. This is due to lack of appeal to the mass audience in cities around the country that promoters like the USHRA regularly visit.

Born of the farmer, and those who owned the 'bragging rights' for their region, the lowly diesel tractor has come a long way from its small cubic inch, 100 horsepower rating and earth-moving duties. Today's competitive Super Stock tractors have been likened to a volcano on wheels as they belch plumes of jet-black diesel smoke some 50 feet above themselves, clawing

and churning their way along the clay track, spinning their 6 foot-tall multi-ply tires at almost 100 miles per hour.

Due to the differences in tractor sizes, the displacements and to the modifications possible to the straight 6-cylinder, V-6 and V-8 engines, the NTPA has divided the tractors into the following classes:

Modified Tractors–Split into 4 weight classes of 5,200lb, 7,200lb, 9,200lb and 11,200lb, this class has little similarity to a real farm tractor as they are commonly built with 2 to 6 V-8 engines each of 500 (and above) cubic inch displacement all nestled closely in one frame. Easily the most powerful vehicles in motor sports, they feature exotic aluminum engines supercharging, fuel injection, explosive alcohol fuels and tires almost six-feet high. In some cases they may be powered by 2 or 3 turbocharged V-12 Allison airplane engines that produce, combined, over 7,000 hp.

Super Stock–With weights from 5,500lb to 11,200lb, this class resembles the original farm tractor. However, their sheetmetal hides hide six-cylinder diesel engines with in-line turbochargers and over 1,200 hp; a far cry from what International Harvester, Ford, John Deere and Allis Chalmers originally built.

Pro Stock–Very similar to the Super Stock class, this tractor has great appeal to those on a racing budget as they are limited to one turbocharger and a smaller tire size. Weight classes are 10,000 and 12,000 lb.

Mini Tractor–Sitting astride the mini tractor has been likened to mounting a bucking Bronco–while it's in motion! With just two competition weights of 1,550 lb and 1,750 lb and a wheelbase of less than eight feet, these tractors are truly a wild ride. Especially since they use the same blown and injected V-8 engines that are common to the powerful modified class tractors.

If the power produced by the modified tractor classes is awe inspiring, then the mini tractor must be the original wild ride itself. Imagine if you can, sitting directly behind a 1,500 hp blown, injected, alcohol-burning, all-aluminum V-8 of approximately 500 cubic inches displacement. When the moment of truth comes with the drop of the starter's flag, you engage the multiple-disc clutch, 'hammer' the gas pedal–and hang on for your life! As you may be thinking, there is little time for error as you steer the tractor the length of the 300-foot track.

Unfortunately, these dynamite packages are only seen at NTPA-sanctioned shows as some show sponsors consider them too great a problem to control for the limited amount of track space at the usual stadium shows.

Amongst the major differences between outdoor and indoor stadium pulls is the distance the vehicle must go to make a 'full pull' of the entire track. The NTPA standard is 300 feet, whereas the indoor shows at major stadiums are usually confined to 150 or 200 feet of track. This allows a shut-down area should a puller do too well, or a mishap takes place. Indoor tracks also make more difficult the sled operator's job; he applies his knowledge differently at shorter tracks.

The sounds of multiple plys of tire cords straining against the well-packed clay track surface, the smell of high-octane fuels and diesel smoke hovering above the track after the Super Stock tractors make their bid, the resonant racket of the valves closing in multiple-engined tractors, as the spent racing fuels exit chromed exhaust stacks, and the roar of the enthusiastic crowds, prepare you for the pulling power of the final attraction that is presented next. No doubt, you can see why the NTPA calls truck and tractor pulling, 'The most powerful motorsport in the world!'

Since the days of the original farm tractor with an implanted V-8 engine, and the days of the original Banter Orange modified (both circa 1974), tractor pulling has become as modern as any motor sport in the world.

▶

Most of the tractors are kept almost as they were built by the factory. Although engine side covers are part of the rules, it's more brand allegiance that the original paint colors are kept.

◀

Smoking like a factory, tire speeds exceeding legal limits, controlling the rear brakes, watching the gages and the track–and still the driver has to see where he's going!

▲

The modern tractor puller. A specially-built machine with factory cover still intact hides enough horsepower to move 40,000 lb down a dirt track. Notice studs in wheel center to hold weights.

Stepping back into history, this photo was taken at one of the earliest Indy Super Pulls. The tall white exhaust pipes, narrow front tire track and overall look, make this tractor 'almost stock' by today's standards.

Facing page, top:
Although this mini-tractor was good at the local levels, it's simple frame and stock Ford engine would not compete with technical attributes of NTPA pullers.

Since this photo of 1981 vintage, Dickie Sullivan and his Big Red IH have gone on to win four Indy Super pull classes, including the 1986 9,500 lb class. The International Harvester tractors seem to be the brand to beat in the heavyweight classes.

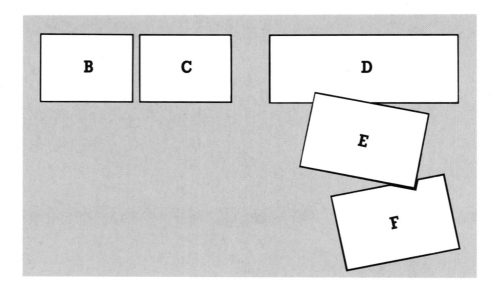

Main photo
A dry track and a quick pull make for a very choking pull for both driver and sled operator.

B
One of the earliest extremely modified pullers, the Banter Brothers established a trend of multiple engines that has no end in sight . . .

C
. . . as their 1986 tractor clearly shows. Their latest is six 500-plus cid V-8s with approximately 1,500 hp per engine.

D
Starting with a mini back in the late 70s, the father and son team of Stan and Johnny Mello, became a powerful mini-tractor team with their Super Fly and Wild Fly tractors that consistently placed in top three places nationally.

E
Leo Kay is another big threat in today's tractor pulling. As almost everyone runs identical engine sizes, it's driver skill that's making the difference. Most of the engines use a constant-flow, alcohol fuel injection with a 6-71 or 8-71 GMC blower for maximum fuel compression. Notice driver's suit and helmet that is becoming a larger part of safety of sport.

F
Weighing in at 7,000 lb, Mike Hoff's Big Blue III took third place in the USHRA for 1986. Powered by three 534 cid Keith Black aluminium engines equalling some 3,600 hp, Mike estimates his tire speeds in excess of 100 mph. Hence the usage of steel screws that all the tractor pullers use to keep their tires on the wheels.

Backing up a low-power V-8 with a healthy alcohol injected V-12 Allison, Bionic Buzzard always carries the tires high down the track.

Caught in action at a regional California pull in 1983, Mike Lorenzo and Dynamite mini-tractor are typical of the variety of driver positions that owners prefer.

LIKE THE HIGH WIRE TRAPEZE ARTIST or the man shot from a cannon during a circus show, every show must have its entertainment features. In pulling, the turbines, jets, funny cars and exhibition vehicles fulfill this scenario.

The invitational vehicles, as they are known, are purely for show. Their task is to awe the viewers with funnels of flame some thirty feet high, to carry their front wheels almost fifteen feet above the track surface the entire 200-feet, or tear-up the clay ground as their tandem driven wheels spin at close to 100mph the full track distance.

IX
Turbines,
Jets & Exhibitionists

They're not there to compete with like vehicles, that is, except for the funny cars (also known as floppers) that can sometimes muster enough vehicles at one event to make a competition viable. This class of pullers are on a never-ending search for something unique in the sport, something that has never been done before. A vehicle that is as close to the limits of sanity as can be made safe before the crowds in a closed stadium. There are few rules governing these vehicles, except that of absolute safety.

At the top of the list of these exhibitions vehicles is the turbine or jet-powered tractor. Curiously enough, just one family has the grip on this unique vehicle. The Arfons family, *Green Monster* Art, son 'turbo' Tim, and daughter, 'Dragon Lady' Dusty, provide one of the most stunning shows in this sport. While Art and Dusty are competing for title and awards in the tractor class, Tim woos the crowds with exhibition runs of his *Starfire* funny car puller.

Back in the late 1950s when drag racing was getting organized, Art Arfons was just experimenting with turbine-powered engines in drag racers. By the mid 60s, Art had set several world land speed records at the Bonneville Salt Flats near Wendover, Utah and went on to set records in both time and speed on the quarter mile drag racing tracks. He was the first person to clock over 200mph in the quarter mile and set an almost 300mph record in 5.5 seconds in that same distance.

By the mid 70s, Art realised that luck may not be with him on his next near-fatal crash at such high speeds, and soon tractor pulling had its first turbine-powered tractor, the Busch *Green Monster.*

It wasn't too many years after that start that Tim and Dusty were doing more than just travelling and helping out with their father's tractor. Tim soon got into IHRA drag racing with a T-58 turbine-powered top fuel racer and has lately joined the tractor ranks with his *Green Monster* and *Starfire* funny cars.

Petite and quiet, Dusty tried her first turbine tractor at the age of eighteen and now drives her own *Dragon Lady* tractor the same 7,200lb weight class as her father's.

Art Arfons *Green Monster:*
Engine: twin GE T-64 turbines (originally from a Sikorsky helicopter).
Horsepower: 6,000 plus at turbine speed of 17,000 rpm's
Gearbox: one-off custom utilizing planetaries and homemade transmission.
Rearend: Standard 23,000lb Rockwell.
Rear Tires: Firestone 30.5L-32 pullers front and 5.00-15 front.
Fuel: diesel or kerosene.

Both Tim and Dusty utilize similar components with the exception that their tractors use a single smaller 1,500 hp GE T-58 turbine, and are equipped with a Lenco transmission and Dana 60-series rear end. The brakes are dual disc styles depending upon weight of tractor. All share rack & pinion steering and same tire sizes.

The family's newest attraction is Tim's Suzuki Quadracer ATV. Powered by the same GE T-58 turbine as his Starfire funny car, the bike is capable of accelerating at 2 g-forces, while attaining speeds three times faster than the Space Shuttle leaving its launch pad. Capable of a 250mph top speed; 'If you stood it one end, there's no doubt it would go straight up till it ran out of fuel,' Tim profoundly tells admirers that ask about power. However, a two-degree downward incline assures that the Quadracer keeps its nose to the ground. Unlike the turbine-powered tractors, this bike uses no transmission or drive components as it's a live jet engine complete with afterburner that produces thunderous 'burner pops' and a 20-foot plume out back. After a short run, the 4-foot parachute and four-wheel disc brakes assure full and safe stopping. However, the turbines are not the final word in pulling power as many of the NTPA and USHRA legends can tell you. Like so many in the pulling sport, Gary Collins comes from a farming background. His daily occupation is in fact a farmer in the state of Colorado, just east of the Continental Divide mountain range. Campaigning both the modified '80 Kenworth truck and the glassfiber-bodied '86 Ford Mustang funny car, Gary and road-going mechanic, Ray, have the distinction of only missing three full pulls in the last several years. That's from a total of over 300 individual pulls!

Named the *Budweiser Boss,* the twin-engined custom truck and its 540cid Keith Black all-aluminium engines create over 2,500 hp that is driven through the latest in pulling technology gearboxes, and the typical Rockwell differential and axle assemblies. The tires are a nominal 18.4 x 16.1 size of Firestone pullers with aluminium wheels for less unsprung weight. The *Avenger* funny car uses a similar powerplant and drive train.

Of the crossovers from the tanks of NHRA drag racing into pulling, Mike Hoff stands near the head of the group. Spending his younger years in drag racing has helped Mike in pulling as he not only campaigns his original triple Hemi-engined tractor, *Big Blue,* but also handles the driving duties of the *Chi-Town Hustler,* a Dodge Daytona funny car exhibition puller.

One of the largest differences between the several classes of tractor pullers is that exhibition class vehicles often cost more to build than a competitive tractor, and several times the cost of a truck. The obvious extra expense is in the construction labour costs of the steel and glassfiber bodies that have to be formed one at a time, which drives exhibition vehicles into the $100,000 region for vehicles like Gary Collin's *Budweiser Boss.* Funny cars often cost over $50,000 if you really want to win some major earnings in return.

Although the exhibition vehicles are definitely not the most powerfully-engined pullers, it's not the power the show promoter is after. What they've really searching for is crowd reaction, the connection with what they see as being unusual, and in some cases what they've driven to the event. As in the case of funny cars and their resemblance to current factory production street-driven cars.

For the exhibition pullers, the future is never certain as someone is always building what could be called 'the bigger and better mousetrap'. However, the class is exciting, well-liked, and along with the TWD class has a very certain steady future in the sport of pulling.

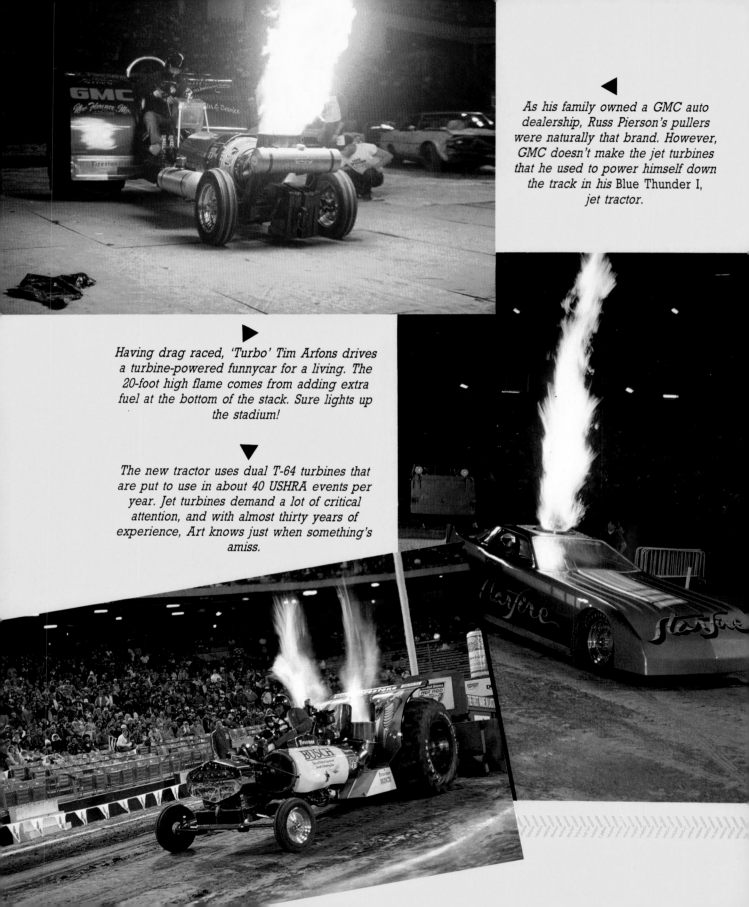

As his family owned a GMC auto dealership, Russ Pierson's pullers were naturally that brand. However, GMC doesn't make the jet turbines that he used to power himself down the track in his Blue Thunder I, jet tractor.

Having drag raced, 'Turbo' Tim Arfons drives a turbine-powered funnycar for a living. The 20-foot high flame comes from adding extra fuel at the bottom of the stack. Sure lights up the stadium!

The new tractor uses dual T-64 turbines that are put to use in about 40 USHRA events per year. Jet turbines demand a lot of critical attention, and with almost thirty years of experience, Art knows just when something's amiss.

▲

Gary Collins' Avenger funnycar, uses a single 540 cid all-aluminum engine, housed under a Mustang glassfiber body with a 125-inch wheelbase.

◄

With dad looking on, Dusty Arfons awaits the final signal for her run down the track. Being the young lady she is, Dusty doesn't always push her tractor as hard as it can go. Notice the use of a full firesuit and safety gear.

▶

The most innovative exhibition truck to come about so far, is no doubt Bob Thompson's Santanimal. Based upon an '85 Ford F-250 pickup, this wheelstander has no transmission, driveshaft, transfer case, differentials or even a suspension system. The truth is, that this truck moves by hydraulics, the transfer of pressurized fluids by use of pumps and servos. The engine provides the power for the main hydraulic pump, and the careful control of fluid allows the truck to turn and wheelstand. The wheelstands we imagine are controlled by a moving weight box in the truck bed. As this system has several possibilities for moving earth and supplies (Bob's company is in that same business) in the frigid climates, Bob isn't giving away any secrets.

▲

The latest Arfons innovation is Tim's Suzuki ATV. It now shoots flame some thirty feet out the tail!

Facing page, top:
One secret to the immense success of Gary's truck puller, is the 170-inch wheelbase that spreads the load further ahead of the pulling hitch. He's missed just three full pulls in the last several years of pulling, an amazing record in itself. A rear view of his new Budweiser Boss puller, shows the 5-ton Rockwell differential and axles, the lack of suspension and Firestone 18.4x16.1 tyres, that are much taller than the usual puller. The front suspension consists of shocks and coil springs.

◀

So that parts supplies aren't too great, the KW and flopper use the same engine configurations. The brakes are a driveline style and the steering system is hydraulic, much like a number of monster trucks.

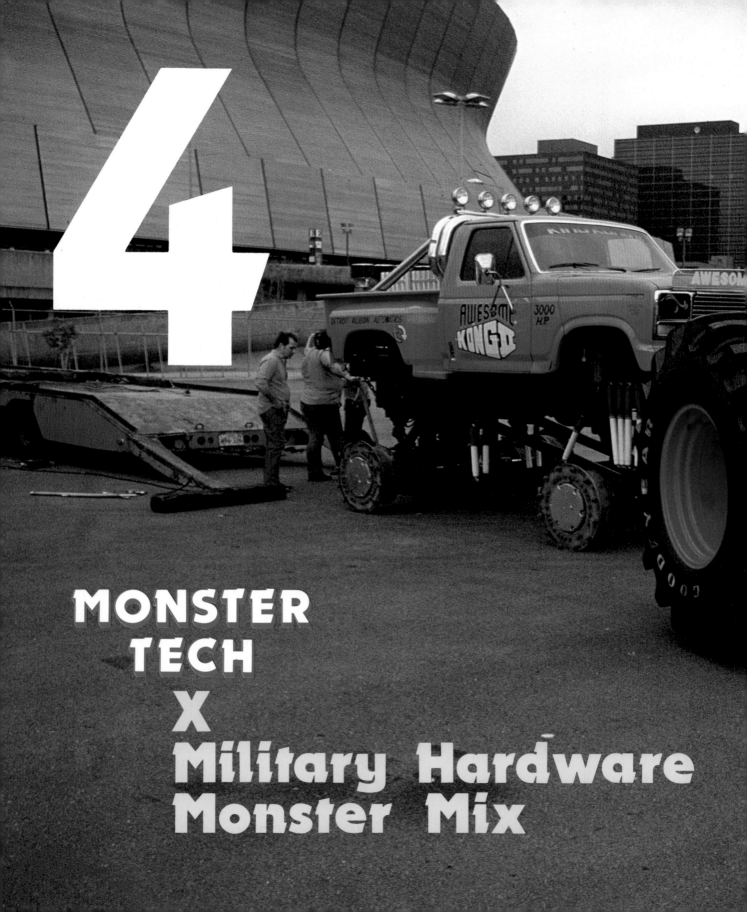

4

MONSTER TECH X Military Hardware Monster Mix

AS THERE ARE NO LIMITS IMPOSED upon how monster trucks are powered, the engines are simply limited by imagination and the builders budget. The word budget, however, is one that has little to do with the building of these projects as the bottom line appears to be no less than $40,000 for the basic parts. That figure–no less–would not include the dressing items, nor labour costs and is predicated upon a fair amount of shopping around. The average cost of a monster truck is approximately $80,000 when labour is included.

As you can see, becoming the master of one of these creations isn't inexpensive. It not only takes a lot of shopping, but several months of sweat and backstrain to complete one that the crowds will accept as a true competitor in this ever-growing field. Not only should the truck be powerful, it looks like the sport is growing into greater showmanship daily, as evidenced by the infinite details on such monsters as *Fly-N-Hi* and *Aces High.*

Building a monster truck is like building any racing vehicle from the ground up, it takes detailed planning, a very full understanding of how parts interact and a full understanding of the overall theories and practices of vehicle suspension. At best, perched on their 72-inch tall tires (that's not including the actual tread cleats) these trucks are top-heavy and have almost no visibility within twenty feet of their front bumper.

The bodystyle used is purely a choice of brand allegiance and personal preference; everything from KW trucks, classic Chevys and Fords and brand new bodies have been used to cover the tremendous drive trains. Of course, to make the theme of a 4x4 truck complete many owners adorn their trucks with chrome winch bumpers, dual winches, several high power off-road lights and body trim items, such as tube grills and chrome rollbars.

Being the control center of the monster, it's purely a matter of choice and function as to how well the cab is laid out with controls. However, most are quite stock as fitting the electrical harness, steering and gearbox controls is not that much of a problem once the truck is completely gutted of all factory installations.

In the case of those trucks using the standard body-on-frame construction, the factory options of power windows, power doorlocks and stereo are often left in as convenience items. Custom seats are a must due to the pounding the driver, and occasional passenger, can undergo.

As safety is the highest priority on the list, many of the teams install a complete 2-inch rollcage inside the stock cab to protect the driver in the event of a rollover. Usually enough, most of the teams use just a single lap belt harness to secure the driver, this is due to the speed and weight involved. At car crushing speeds, the speed is not dangerous, but with weights in the 15,000 lb area, just the momentum the vehicle can have is enough severely to crush most cabs and bed-mounted rollbars. In reality, the rollbars are really there from which to hang flags and the high-powered lights, not to act as a safety item.

On the other hand, with those trucks that engineer 'clamshell' type bodies, the cockpit is a whole different story. The floor, dashboard and all the factory parts are discarded in favor of a steel floor, custom aluminum dash with necessary instruments installed and two racing bucket seats with harnesses. The rollcage is sometimes built into the cab structure, but most seem to depend upon the bed-mounted bar. Not the safest bet considering these trucks are now racing around the arenas and not just slowly crushing cars!

Obviously, the most important asset for these vehicles is a very potent engine: even two of them in the case of *Mega Force.* In this game however, 400 cubic inch engines are considered small as the usual is 500 plus. *Bigfoot I* has the most cubes in a monster truck with its Alan Root-built all-aluminum 640 inch V-8. Yes, that's over 10 litres of stump-pulling power with a 1,500 hp ability.

Most of the engines used are Chevrolet or

Ford-based V-8s with steel blocks and aluminum heads. If they're not supercharged with the use of the GMC crank-driven 'blower', they're turbocharged with dual turbos or equipped with constant flow racing fuel injection. Of course, there are those like *Rollin' Thunder,* the original *King Kong* and *Boss Hog* that have chosen to use in-line 6-cylinder diesels due to the power band that's available at very low rpm. These heavy duty engines also last several times longer than most of the V-8s. Monster trucking is not inexpensive as we've said!

Many engines use dual racing-prepared Predator variable venturi carburetors as they're able to handle the constant sloshing around of the fuel and other detrimental effects these trucks undergo while racing. Depending upon the association they run with, the use of alcohol, aviation fuels and racing fuels are used. Nitromethane is strictly forbidden due to its volatility and the confined area. Nitrous oxide is used by many of the mud racing trucks, but only small-volume bottles are used.

Although it takes power to move the enormous weight of these trucks, it's not the engine that does all the work. The reasons for the success of these heavy-weights is their usage of the military drive train and related components that not only provide the ability for the stunts, but also account for their huge weights. The integration and variety of military and farming components is as varied as the colors of the trucks themselves.

Once the power exits the engine it usually enters an automatic transmission that originated at Ford or Chevrolet. In some cases, owners have chosen to use Detroit Allisons and a variable gearbox, especially with diesel engines. By running the transmission into two separate inline transfer cases that have different ratios, the overall gearing ratio can be lowered significantly. This allows gearing so low, that some of the monsters literally crawl along. This tremendous torque is often required for bus crushing and sled pulling.

Although there is no standard transfer case, the usual is the military version of the Rockwell 2 1/2-ton or the 5-ton version. Others have used New Process 203s, NP 205s, air actuated earth-moving transmissions and even complicated gear reduction units combined with quick change gear ratios.

The axles and differentials used by most are also Rockwell military units with a 5-ton rating, although this original trend is changing to other brands and styles. There are several reasons for using these huge axles: strength, the ability to fit enormous wheels, and the location of the pinion gear. In order to perform some of the stunts with a large margin of safety and longevity of components, the differentials had to be large. Large differentials have large axles that carry greater weight as well as larger hubs to mount those huge tires. It's as though these axles were made for monster trucks as they provide the height, strength and awe that these trucks are looking for.

The unique feature of the military differential is its pinion gear location and ensuing angle of driveshaft connection. As the military rear end is designed with a top-loading style of axle drive, this allows for a lesser driveshaft angle thereby lessening U-joint problems with such horsepower.

A side benefit that has evolved from these differentials is the disc brake location that many have engineered to be used off the rear of the pinion drive. Using a four-piston caliper with metallic pads, these custom-made conversion brake systems

As those tall tires present problems with bridges and exceed width laws in most states, many of the trucks are trailered with standard truck tyres. Kevin Dabney even made his own steel wheels to mount onto his 20-ton axles.

One of the first problems once the truck is unloaded, is the fitting of the huge tires. Just getting the axles propped-up is a feat in itself.

offer such tremendous stopping power that they can strain the drive axles.

As most of these monsters compete in races and are attaining speeds of up to 30 mph, the braking systems have had to come a long way since the military designers sketched them on paper. Stock, they were a typical four-wheel drum arrangement we're all used to seeing. This however, has been changed by almost everyone except for the Bigfoot trucks that use their own system that works very well on stock-appearing military brakes.

The most common sight for monster brakes are a single or twin aluminum air tanks that help power the 5-ton dual master cylinders and military Hydro-Vac or hydraulically-assisted power brakes that help stop these heavyweights.

Like all 4x4 vehicles, these huge axles feature the choice of full-time or part-time hub engagement depending upon the use of hub styles. The newest system that has greatly helped lessen axle breakage is the planetary drive type of gear set.

As even these huge differentials can only fit a gear as low as 10.26:1, using the two speeds of the transfer case often makes the overall driven ratio of these trucks very sluggish. This sometimes manifests itself in a 'loose' drive train that often damages axles, according to Bigfoot. By welding a planetary gear set to each axle (that consists of the axle spline driving a sun gear which in turn drives several planetary gears), the problem of frequent axle breakage is almost a thing of the past. The penalty for this good fortune however, is a 300lb weight increase per set of gears, which is multiplied by four axles. It also lessens the wheel speed that is useful for mudbogs. It does however, greatly increase engine speed.

Of course, with such weight to carry, the springs and shocks are vital to controlling these trucks. One thing you may have spotted is the overabundance of shock absorbers (or dampeners, which ever philosophy suits you). As Jim Kramer, main driver of the Bigfoot trucks says, 'When we were crushing cars, shocks were just for aesthetics, they were just hung there. Now, they have to work'. And work they do. Like desert racing trucks, many monsters are equipped with a nominal four shocks per axle that in conjunction with leaf springs do a well orchestrated job of controlling their gyrations during hard landings. The use of two to three dozen shocks is more advertising than actual suspension design. Of course, depending upon how hard the truck is driven and its total weight, twenty shocks seem to be the normal amount that most trucks use.

One of the more innovative suspension systems used is that of air bags as pioneered by *Ms. Bigfoot* and the Dabney brothers' *Blue Thunder* Camaro. Utilizing air bags, their accompanying air tanks and the pump systems from commercial applications have allowed a tuneable suspension that to some extent has had success but still requires a few more shocks than is wanted. *Ms. Bigfoot* uses fourteen, *Blue Thunder* (now *Thunder Beast*) uses a total of forty. They are, however, about 7,000lb apart, and *Thunder* is driven with a lot more aggression than *Ms* has ever seen.

Although these giant-sized tires are used primarily to gain height, they also have a large task in suspension control due to their inflation and absorption characteristics. The standard Goodyear Terra tires as used by Bigfoots are just 6-ply construction as they were originally designed for fertilizer spreading and to

▶

Although some trucks use a twin steering ram-style of hydraulics, it depends partially upon the ram and the pressure behind it just how fast the steering is and how many seconds it takes to go 'lock-to-lock'. Here, Samson I uses a single ram to turn both wheels that are connected with a large steel tie-rod . . .

▼

. . . which allows Don to turn his tires at about 45-degrees from the straight ahead position.

In some cases, it seems monster trucks become a four-wheeled billboard for shock manufacturers. Clydesdale has forty Rancho brand in total.

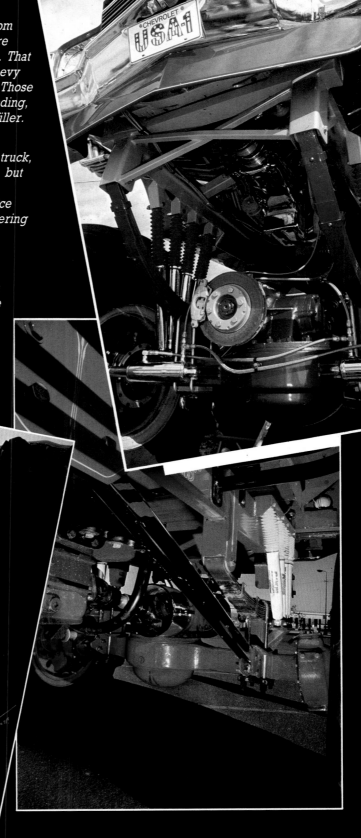

▶ *Aces High* uses dual steering rams from heavy-duty mining equipment, that are controlled with an Orbital steering pump. That eases the load on driver, and stock Chevy steering pump; a well-integrated system. Those smoothed welds took two months of grinding, and are not achieved by using a putty filler.

▼ Being from a 'show' background with his truck, Bob Holman's *Beast* not only has beauty, but function also. He uses lots of steel reinforcement as well as chrome. Notice steering column and pump that feeds steering rams.

Hot Stuff *Jeep* uses a $2^1/2$-ton transfer case (in blue at left) to drive a short driveshaft to 5-ton Rockwell differential. Notice the usage of large locating bar, four shocks and leaf spring suspension. Due to height of the Jeep, the angle of driveshaft is almost straight, which is what most owners want for longevity.

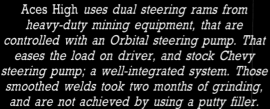

123

leave almost no impression upon the ground travelled. *Bigfoot* standard inflation is less than 10psi as the tires are used as part of the suspension system. On the other hand, the Firestones, as used by the Dabney brothers, are 12-ply tires that were built for mining. As Kevin Dabney and Jim Kramer told us, the more the tire plys, the lesser the cushion upon returning to Earth. The final point of monstrous details is the ability to steer with both axles. Although the first systems were salvaged from tractors and commercial trucks, the steering systems of today are a far cry from the automotive type that uses a hydraulic pump with Pitman Arm and drag link.

One effective system used is the orbital steering design that allows a large hydraulic pump to replace the power steering reservoir and low-pressure pump. By using a high pressure pump (as much as 2,000 psi) that supplies approximately 8 gallons-per-minute flow, a several gallon reservoir, two or four hydraulic rams, high-pressure hydraulic line and a hefty electrical alternator/battery system, most monsters can be steered with an amazing ease. In fact, some of them have a turning radius as tight as any large US sedan. The rear steering is usually accomplished with electrically-operated hydraulics that are actuated by a momentary contact switch that most owners mount on the driver's door. This allows the driver to look out of the truck while actuating the rear steering if necessary.

What actually makes the steering very technical is the correct valving, the pumps and the rams themselves. All three of these components have to be matched correctly for optimum safety as just a tad too much speed in the valving for the rear steering can have disastrous results that could endanger both driver and spectator.

Some interesting monster facts are:

–*Awesome King* weighs approximately 21,000lb, whereas *Ms. Bigfoot* weighs less than 9,000lb. The average monster weight is about 14,000lb. *Bigfoot V* shod with eight tires weighs in at almost 30,000lb.

–*Awesome Kong's* V-12 Allison engine uses 33 gallons of engine coolant.

–Heights range from about 9 feet (with 48 inch tires) to just under 16 feet (measured at lightbar) for *Bigfoot V* with its ten foot-tall tires.

–When equipped with four 74x44 inch tires the S-10 *Bear Foot* is almost twenty feet wide. However, *Bigfoot V* with its eight ten foot-tall tires measures in at nearly 22 feet.

–Depending upon the plys, large monster tires weigh approximately 800lb apiece. Their steel rims weigh almost 1,000lb, whereas aluminum decreases the weight to 750lb. This makes most complete wheels about 1,800lb.

–Cost on these tires runs from $1,500 for the small 48s to $4,000 per tire for the large 73s. The rims can cost $2,000 a set for steel and $6,000 for a lightweight aluminum set. Totals of $15,000 are not uncommon as shipping is always very expensive.

As for weight, how about 5-ton axles that weigh in at over 2,000lb and transfer cases and planetary gears that weigh over 300lb apiece. Of course, the axles can be lightened by 1,000lb apiece if the drum brakes and backing plates are removed in favor of driveline-style disc brakes.

–The 70-ton-rated differentials for *Awesome Kong* weigh 3,200 lb apiece, and cost over $30,000 each. The drive train is so specialized that there's several brands used as well as custom pieces made by a military hardware supplier. Luckily, much of the work was sponsored.

–As for costs, how about: $2,000 apiece for 5-ton military axles; $2,000 per pair for 2¹/₂-ton axles; $2,000 for a 2¹/₂-ton military transfer case; and then there's the steering system, electrical, body, paint, and trailer for hauling your beast.

Like the old saying goes 'the difference between men and boys is the price of their toys!'

The original Rockwell military axles use a standard brakedrum on axle design that adds about 620 lb per drum and backing plate assembly. This is one reason many owners convert to the driveline disc-brakes that are shown.

Most of the monster truck frames are built from 3/8 or 1/4-inch steel, that's why the finished trucks weigh over 12,000 lb. Notice the use of the dual master cylinder brake reservoirs and heavy-duty steering adaptation.

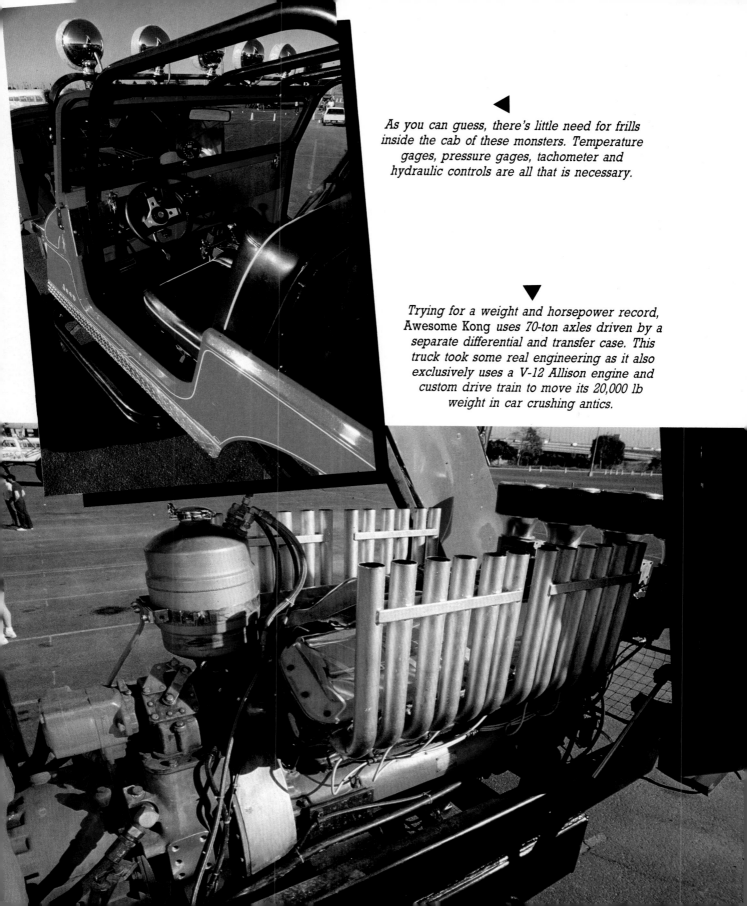

As you can guess, there's little need for frills inside the cab of these monsters. Temperature gages, pressure gages, tachometer and hydraulic controls are all that is necessary.

Trying for a weight and horsepower record, Awesome Kong uses 70-ton axles driven by a separate differential and transfer case. This truck took some real engineering as it also exclusively uses a V-12 Allison engine and custom drive train to move its 20,000 lb weight in car crushing antics.

Like many of the monster trucks, Bear Foot
uses planetary gears to attain an even lower
gear ratio than the stock 5-ton Rockwell axles
will allow. Top speed of some of the trucks is a
maximum 40 mph.

The Rockwell 5-ton military differential is standard monster equipment. Nominal suspension consists of four shocks, leaf springs, a ladder-bar (entering from left side of photo) to tie the axle to the truck body, and an enormous steel liftblock that raises the suspension for greater tire clearance. Warn is the only manufacturer of the locking hubs for monster trucks.

Most of the monster trucks use the bed to locate the dual heavy-duty marine batteries, the small fuel tank and the hydraulic pumps. Here in Samson 1, two lines go to the rear axles for turning ability and the control cable . . .

. . . goes into the cab center, where Don Maples can control the 'crabbing' motion. Notice his cab is in very stock trim, except for the extra gages and fire extinguisher.

Although this engine now uses a blower to make even greater power than the Hilborn injection fitted here, it's quite able to move anything in its way. Notice that the hood continues the use of steel tube, that ties the entire truck together.

Notice this truck has no rear steering ability due to the absence of hydraulic ram and knuckles. Needing height for tire clearance during landings, it was necessary to elevate the shock mounts 1 foot.

The engines used are all part of the attraction of these performers. Although each brand of truck uses its own brand of engine, the ways in which they're used is made for the particular vehicle. The most unusual engine is Skoal Bandit's V-12 Jaguar with Weber carburetors. Much more than 600 hp can be useless in car crushing, but is always needed when pulling the sled.

X1
Muscle Madness – blowers, alchohol & cubes

IF YOU'RE AROUND TRUCK AND
tractor pulling for any length of time, you
soon learn that unlike most other motor
sports that require lightweight engines and
chassis, the sport of pulling reads from a
different rulebook. In fact, their sport is
built around one simple creed: there is no
substitute for cubic inches–bigger is always
better!

Although not a newly discovered motor
sport, pulling is still very much in its
childhood, both in its technical aspects and
in the public's awareness. Like in the
fledgling days of so many other motor
sports, some of the parts used for these
unique vehicles are one-off parts
handmade by individual owners. Fellow
competitors saw how these parts could fit
their 'rig' and somehow a business is born.
Showing their heritage, some of the parts
like tires, wheels, basic engines and drive
train components are readily adaptable for
use with some of the tractors, due to the
original heavy-duty intentions of farming.
However, that doesn't mean that trucks or
tractors are inexpensive to build or
maintain. They're not. With prices that do
not include the basic tractor, even the

lower-powered Pro Stock can have prices
of $20,000 attached to it. For the nationally
competitive multi-engined heavyweights,
the ticket price rises to $100,000,
depending upon how much can be
engineered by the team itself.

The 'judge and jury' as the pulling sled
side has been called, always has the last
word in this sport. For when all is said and
done, the competitors aren't really pulling
against each other, they're matching their
muscle against the weight of the sled. It's
basically a flat bed trailer with 4
non-driving wheels at the rear of it,
together with a large weighted box that is
moved by gears and chains from its start
point at the rear towards the front of the
bed. As the 'pull' tune advances, this
weighted box is bought to bear over a
steel plate (located at ground level) that is
creating friction with the track surface. The
operator can vary the speed of this moving
box according to track surface and length,
the class of pulling vehicle and the
requirements of each race.

It takes considerable skill to manage this
sled as in many cases the operator can
make or break a pull. For instance; during
eliminations the sled weight is moved
faster than during previous rounds so as to
halt the competitors faster, thereby
eliminating everyone except the strongest
that may return for finals, known as
pull-offs.

Unlike monster trucks and exhibition
vehicles that really have few technical
regulations to comply with, the pulling
truck/tractor has hundreds of such rules, as
they are true competition vehicles. As was
explained earlier, as these vehicles fit into
several divisions and classes, there is not
enough space to give blow-by-blow
descriptions of rules and technical
requirements within this book.

Like the building of any finely detailed chassis and drive train for a racing vehicle, the art of building a containment vessel for these extremely powerful machines has come a long way since the days of the essential farm tractor or that of the diminutive garden tractor. Alloys such as Chrome Moly steel, Aluminium, Magnesium and other lightweight metals are all part of today's pulling machinery just as they are in high speed auto racing.

Most of the frames for tractors are constructed of either mild steel plate or Chrome Moly steel, use of which depends upon budget, class of competition and type of vehicle. Many of the frames used by trucks are based upon the factory steel design that has been gusseted for extra strength. On the other hand, if the truck is going to be really competitive, a full custom frame and chassis is just part of the starting budget.

There are bare comforts in any of these vehicles, they are absolutely spartan and designed for racing. Therefore, they have but one seat, a custom electrical harness and the bare necessities that will power the vehicle. A far cry from the way the factory made some of the trucks with all those convenience options, especially if you've bought a new truck and then tore it down to make a fresh up-to-date pulling truck. All of them contain safety systems such as harnesses, fire extinguishers, fuel cells, containment blankets for the transmissions in case of explosion, electrical system kill switches and even reversing lamps for reversing indication to the sled operator. All drivers wear helmets and fireproof clothing in NTPA sanctioned racing.

The engines used in truck and tractor pulling are the epitomy of brute force. Like an Olympic athlete, they're bred for one reason only; in this case, huge amounts of torque at 8,000 rpm engine speeds. Most run alcohol or racing fuels of 120 or greater octane rating, which allows 1,000 hp from injected V-8 engines and 1,500 hp from fuel injected and blown V-8s. The 2,700 hp from fuel-injected and supercharged V-12 Allison aircraft engines, that displace 1,710 cubic inches, reminds you of standing beside a WWII aircraft awaiting take-off.

With the variety of engines based on the legendary Chevrolet and Ford V-8 engine blocks, pushing as much as 600 cubic inches and 1,700 hp, the use of earplugs at the starting line of some tractor pulls is part of self-preservation.

One of the most interesting aspects of pulling is the innovation applied to the transmissions and (4x4) transfer cases. Unlike the monster trucks, the pulling pieces are usually lightweight, non-military hardware made specifically for this sport.

Quickchange aluminum cases with hardened gear ratios that are changeable within minutes is the asset that many pullers are looking for in these $2,000 transmissions. Of course, on the local and regional competition levels, these specialized pieces may rarely be seen.

The differentials are often names like Hallibrand, Franklin, SCS, Dana and 2-ton rated units that have a military origin. The axles are the fully locked style as used in drag racing, as there is no reason for allowing differential slip to occur in straight line driving.

The most intriguing technical aspect of multi-engined tractors is a major innovation called the 'Crossbox,' an invention credited to Carl Bosse. The crossbox is the transmission (or gearbox, if you wish) that combines the output of two engines into one common shaft. As the NTPA Unlimited Class tractors are sporting two and three

138

◄

For weight and safety, many of the teams locate their batteries out front as this allows easier access. The design of the weight box is purely personal, but cleanliness helps when you're sponsored.

Known technically as drawbars, the sanctioning associations have definitive material requirements, heights, and construction standards for the hitch that attaches to the sled. For those with a discerning eye, you will also see the kill switch wire that attaches to the sled. During a pull, if the puller becomes detached from sled for some reason, this kills all power. If you look over this truck's tire closely, you'll notice that it's had some custom grooving done to suit the needs of the owner.

▼

◄ & ◄

The placement of the weights is usually done on a 60/40 bias. However, that's just a starting point, for each track is different and knowledge of such is where matches are won.

V-12s, and four (or more) 500 cid engines, the crossbox is crucial to today's pullers. Possibly the most difficult aspect of driving a tractor puller is in its braking requirements. Not only does the driver have to control the throttle pedal, but also has independent braking controls for each of the rear tires. While twisting its way down the 300 feet of track, the Mini tractor-driver often has to use this system to control the rapid side movements that allow drifting from the straight line that is best for top speed. No wonder they are called the wildest ride in pulling.

One less worry for the puller is the relative lack of suspension that is used. The rear axles are solid-mounted in what is called a 'hardtail' suspension that lacks springs and shock absorbers. On the other hand, the front axles require suspension due to the placement of the engine and additional weight that is required to aid traction.

Unique to pulling is the use of very special tires and their ability to be cut to order for individual tracks and surfaces. 'Grooving' as it's called, is a very difficult operation of removing and/or sharpening the existing tire lugs (knobby treads) that can often make the difference between a good pull and spinning the tires enough to dig holes in the track.

Some interesting truck and tractor puller facts are:

–Short blocks for mild engines cost $3,000.
–Crankshafts cost $1,500.
–Transmissions cost $2,500.
–Huge 8 liter racing engines cost $15,000.
–Truck puller tires cost from $250 to $500.
–A race-ready V-12 Allison can cost $15,000 and yet a rebuildable jet turbine can cost as little as $3,000. It is however, the high parts prices and the lack of knowledge about these V-12 engines that keep them from competition.

–The speed of mini tractor tires can exceed 120 mph.

–Funny cars in tractor pulling cannot possibly compete at drag strips as the engine is placed too far forward and the frame is built too rugged and heavy for use in that sport.

–The wheelbase of truck pullers vary from 130 to 170 inches, depending upon the builders design.

–The large tractor tire/wheel combination weighs approximately 350 lb, of which the alloy wheel weighs only 62 lb. Some rims use as many as 12 wheel studs on the axle.

–To stop the spinning of the tire on the wheel, sheet metal screws are installed in the wheels and through the tires. Depending upon the tire size, as many as 130 screws can be used on a wheel.

–The NTPA is one of very few motor sports to have a safety record of fifteen years without any major participant injuries.

After a pull has finished, the track crew mark the finish position at the front of the sled which is then measured by more officials and recorded on the logs. The measurements have to be precise down to the inch, as money rides on that crucial figure.

If you want to win big money at pulling against top guns like Jim Brockmann, the engines to use are as exotic as technology gets. All-out, aluminium race engines equipped with a 8-71 GMC 'blower' and maximum fuel injection, good for about 3,000 cfm of air gulping, cost about $30,000 each. Sponsors are absolutely necessary.

Representative of the modern mini-tractor, Johnny Mello's '82 Super Fly uses a built-in fuel tank out front, small tires with aluminum wheels, lacks front brakes and uses no front suspension. The frame is aluminum. Capable of producing over 1,000 hp, the Rodeck 588 cid engine features all the newest racing components backed by a twin-disc clutch, scattershield and special SCS 2-speed gearbox. The differential is a modified Dana 60-series with 4:10 ratio gears. As tractors use their brakes to steer, the mini has large discs with twin-piston calipers. All told, it's a $25,000 investment.

Representative of a high quality truck engine
compartment, you'll notice there are several
safety features built into the engine bay. The
fuel tank is away from the driver and located
close to the engine as this setup is using a
constant-flow, crank-driven fuel pump; the
weights are located in a box, not strapped onto
a bar; the mandatory shielding is in place
alongside the engine block, just in case of
thrown connecting rods; all lines are steel
braided style, and not just high-pressure
organic hose; and all control buttons are
located within easy reach of the right hand.

▶

This grooving process has definite assets, and
like most motorsport tires, the track can be
checked for the pattern desired. Notice the
alternating pattern of lugs.

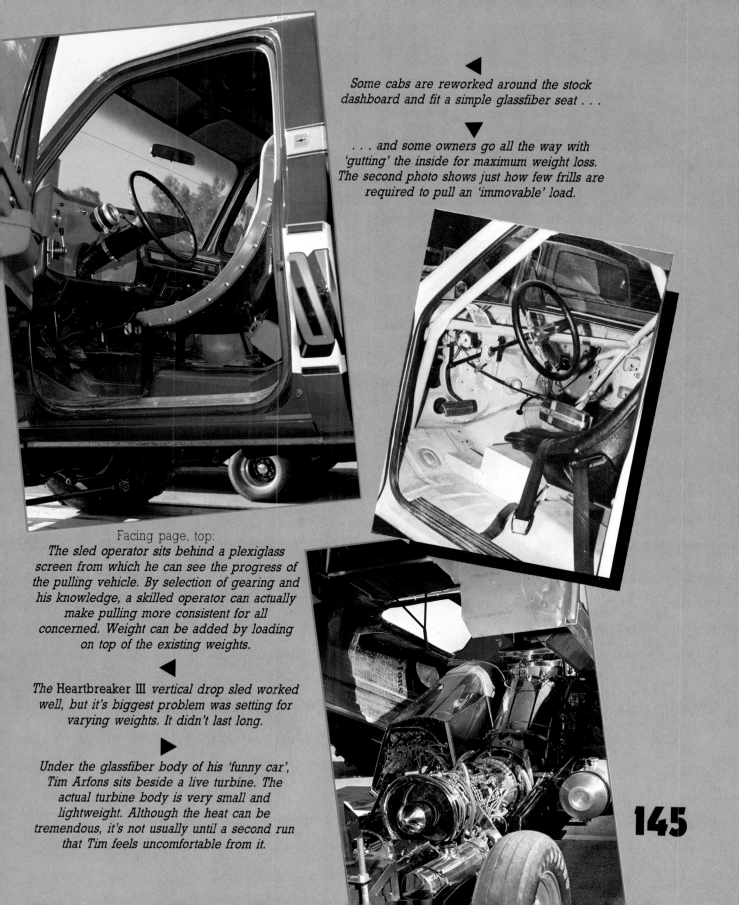

Some cabs are reworked around the stock dashboard and fit a simple glassfiber seat . . .

. . . and some owners go all the way with 'gutting' the inside for maximum weight loss. The second photo shows just how few frills are required to pull an 'immovable' load.

Facing page, top:
The sled operator sits behind a plexiglass screen from which he can see the progress of the pulling vehicle. By selection of gearing and his knowledge, a skilled operator can actually make pulling more consistent for all concerned. Weight can be added by loading on top of the existing weights.

The Heartbreaker III vertical drop sled worked well, but it's biggest problem was setting for varying weights. It didn't last long.

Under the glassfiber body of his 'funny car', Tim Arfons sits beside a live turbine. The actual turbine body is very small and lightweight. Although the heat can be tremendous, it's not usually until a second run that Tim feels uncomfortable from it.

145

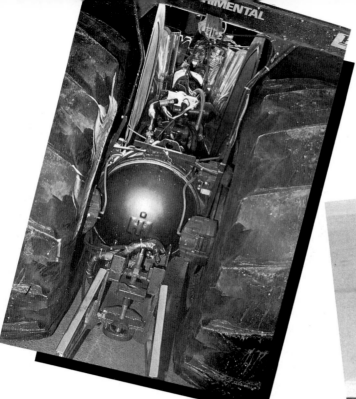

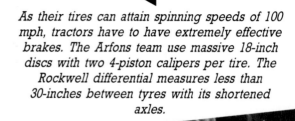

As their tires can attain spinning speeds of 100 mph, tractors have to have extremely effective brakes. The Arfons team use massive 18-inch discs with two 4-piston calipers per tire. The Rockwell differential measures less than 30-inches between tyres with its shortened axles.

To move his tractor around, Art Arfons uses a small motorcycle engine that drives the same system as the turbines during a pull.

Mounted in-between two blast furnaces, there are two brake pedals, a hand-held throttle and gages for turbine monitoring. For safety, sheet steel is used as a floorbase.

XII

On The Road Again

WHETHER YOUR SPORT USES A BALL, a bat, or a board or requires being seated for long periods of time, all competitors know that capturing that elusive title of champion takes time and energy.
In motor sports, most of that time is spent behind the wheel of the tow trailer, and most of the energy is spent putting the vehicle together. After which, the crew has to once again ready themselves to climb behind the steering wheel of the tow trailer, driving ever onwards to the next show date.

In the case of monster truck teams, there is no trophy, award or title – there is no such highly esteemed position as 'National Champion'–yet! The teams travel to points across the North American Continent purely at the invitation of those show promoters that choose to invite them to appear in their events. There are but a handful of trucks that have seasonal or yearly contract dates with nationwide promoters. Most of the teams make their commitments a few months at a time, hoping that while travelling they can get local dates at car dealerships, auto parts stores grand openings or do a promotion in conjunction with the event promoters that will pull more people to that weekend's show.

Monster trucking is expensive to get into, and the monetary rewards for many of the owners is small. Less than a dozen name trucks will have incomes in the six figure ($100,000) bracket. When the year's travel fees, hotels, food, salary and money for broken parts are totalled, there will be very few that will be able to proclaim they have made any money at all.

Some of the largest expenses of being 'on the road' with large trucks like these is the taxation for fuel and commercial licences that each state has on vehicles of a commercial nature. One of the ways in which a few teams deal with this is to mount sleeping quarters onto the tractor/trailer or tow their monster with a motorhome. Depending upon how everything is set up, this allows a personally-owned look that removes them from commercial categories. Of course, a knowledge of the laws of the road for each state always helps alleviate getting costly vehicle violation fines.

The main months for the stadium shows that feature monster trucks, pullers and

such vehicles, runs from about early Fall to late Spring seasons for most of the larger promoters like SRO/Pace, which organizes such meets under the USHRA (United States Hot Rod Assoc.) banner. Of course, because of the high investment, the trucks sit idle as little as possible.

Of all the trucks that I've seen prolifically, the Dabney brothers seem to criss-cross this nation the most. One weekend in San Francisco, California, the next in Seattle, Washington, and the next they were destined for New Orleans, Louisiana. Their home is in North Carolina, as are their families.

Teams such as Golden State Promotions Skoal Bandit and Copenhagen Crusher trucks also seem to travel extensively. With Steve Helm and Gerry Sartin as the

two-man team that drive and travel with these two trucks, life is not easy considering the hours on the highways and the setup that's required.

However, not all trucks tour extensively. For those leaders in this industry we've shown you, life on the road is just part of their greater business. Many own off-road shops, recreational repair businesses or are actively engaged in an automotive repair of some form. For some like Bob Holman, Earl Dagit and Bob Thompson monster trucks are a family affair that grew from personal interests.

The monster mudder trucks like *Cyclops, Mud Lord,* and a few others that have gained national notoriety, travel a little, but are usually regional. The assorted trucks, VW-powered rails and such, are purely local competitors that rarely travel more than a few hundred miles for some good muddy fun. The financial rewards are very little.

One of the leading, and most professional teams, is that of Gerry Sartin (Skoal Bandit) and Steve Helm (Copenhagen Crusher), who drive for Seth Doulton of Golden State Promotions. A businessman by nature, Seth Doulton was one of the first to follow the leading innovators into sponsorships and approaching monster trucking as a business, not as a part-time money-making venture, as seen by some. Sponsored by The US Tobacco Co., Goodyear Tire Co., and several smaller sponsors, the team exhibits their trucks at county fairs, shopping malls, and even the Indianapolis 500 race. This is in addition to mud bogs and monster races that take place all year.

One of the reasons for trucks and tractor pulling becoming such a major motor sport so fast, can be partially attributed to the loss of so many drag racing tracks in the past few years. In Southern California alone two tracks, Orange County International Raceway and Terminal Island Raceway, have closed in the past three years. The imminent closure of Riverside International Raceway, a major racetrack for NASCAR and other national auto events, is just another victim caused by the ever-increasing population problem of Southern California that may eventually put drag racing out of business in that state.

▲

A stadium show presented by SRO/Pace (under their USHRA banner) in the Seattle Kingdome, uses a single mudpit, two sets of car to be crushed for each monster truck, and a 150-foot pulling track. The setup of this show is relatively simple due to the concrete flooring.

◀

On the other hand, the two-day event at Anaheim Stadium in southern California, took days to get ready and was built on an open-air baseball field. Viewed from behind home plate, the two pulling tracks run alongside first and third base lines. The twin mudpits run through the centre of the stadium field and competitors are kept at the rear of the stadium. The cars to be crushed are kept at the sidelines, until they're dragged onto the pulling tracks for competition. The stadium will seat about 45,000 people each night of the event.

Many of the truck and tractor pullers are farmers by occupation. To some of them, pulling came as an alternative to drag racing. To many others, they were drag racers that could no longer afford their sport or couldn't compete at the level they wanted to due to travel requirements. Like the international Grand Prix circuits, NASCAR, and the numerous road-racing associations throughout the world, the NTPA is a true racing association with regional and national champions. Divided into six regions, each has its own champions that can also compete on the national level. With cash prizes and contingency money (money given by manufacturers of auto products that is awarded to winners using their products) at some national events totalling over $100,000, it's easy to see that there is some well-earned cash available at NTPA-sanctioned pulls.

Being the type of racing association they are, spread out around the nation and hosting events on many weekends, the title of USHRA National Champion is not easy to win. As one example, the USHRA often has three events going on in one weekend alone, all of which have varying audiences of 15,000 to 50,000 people.

One of the largest facets in motor sports are the sponsors, for without sponsorship the far greater percentage of auto racing could not even be planned, yet alone actually take place. There is no doubt that beer and tobacco products are the largest sponsors of American motor sports. The sponsorship of the NTPA by tobacco, farming products, motor oil and racing engine parts not only produces sales for the sponsors products, but also makes the cash awards programs very lucrative.

In the USHRA, it's the Ford/Budweiser points competition that provides the largest monetary rewards. Since 1983, this major auto manufacturer and best-selling beer have co-sponsored thirty-two events nationwide for trucks and tractors in two classes. The points champion receives a cash prize and a new Ford truck. Places are given through twelfth position so that even those not so fortunate have some pocket change at season's end.

As the interest grows worldwide in monster trucks and truck and tractor pulling, so will the media coverage. Although monster trucks are competing with each other for cash awards, it's not conceivable that there will be any major media coverage on this entertainment in the near future. Even though there are two monster trucks in Europe and one in Australia, it's doubtful this idea will spread like wildfire. It's too uniquely American, besides being too expensive.

However, the sport of truck and tractor pulling has proven to be a real 'hot item' with the European racing enthusiast. As evidenced by several dozen Europeans visiting the '87 Indy Super Pull, chapters in Great Britain, The Netherlands and West Germany rapidly growing, and requests by European promoters for visits by certain teams, the future of pulling seems to be well imbedded into the world racing community.

What started as a simple bet, a challenge between two farmers, has caught on with racing enthusiasts worldwide. A simple challenge of moving the immovable with a small, but powerful machine. Who ever thought the lowly farm tractor or utility pickup truck would ever gain such status?

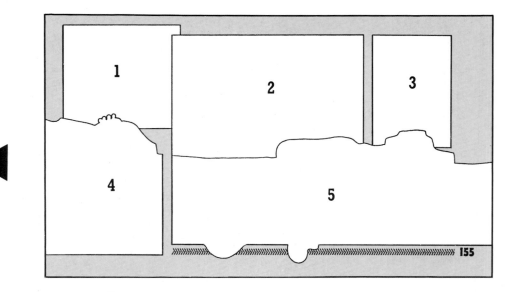

1

Not all trucks are towed in the expensive way of leading names. Making their first show, the Leadfoot team just loaded everything on a trailer and battled the snow storms for several hours.

2

When he travels from his Washington State home, Mike Welch and crew of two are real busy preparing his Super Pete *and* Monster Mash *trucks. With several video credits to the name, they're going to be even busier.*

3

Although the well-known monster trucks are paid well for their antics at stadium shows, a great part of their cash flow comes from the sale of T-shirts, hats, posters and other take-home goodies that are sold at the stadium shows.

4

If you're really interested in getting some sponsorship, getting those tires waxed is just one more job that has to be done to show that professional touch.

5

Brian Shell has kept his '78 Ford Bronco on the road forty-five weeks a year for the past two years. With an investment of $125,000, Brian often has to criss-cross the country to attend events so that sponsor commitments are kept.

As you can see, the trailer rig is a tight fit that leaves only several inches clearance for the tires.

▲

Arriving with two trucks and eight tires in tow, it will be several hours before the guys have finished assembling the trucks and give both of them a thorough cleaning.

▼

Most of the top teams like the 'Inlaws & Outlaws' pulling team use a covered trailer for the trucks, while the semi-tractor rig has a built-in sleeper cab. With national travel and many weeks on the road, the expense of hotel rooms can easily chew on the company profits.

157

Glossary

AR, Arias, Donovan, Keith Black, Milodon, Rodeck: All brand names of extremely powerful racing V-8s that usually exceed 500 cubic inches.

Birdcatcher fuel injection (FI): A fuel injector system so named due to its size of opening, that is big enough to catch birds.

Blown: An expression used to denote an engine that is supercharged by the crank-driven forced induction method. Usually a GMC-derived design that compresses air and fuel into the combustion chamber under greater force than would normal carburetion with normal atmospheric pressures.

CFM: Cubic foot per minute. A measure of air taken into a carburetor per minute.

Dual quads: Dual 4-barrel carburetors. Quad being four, dual quads being two such carburetors.

Flopper: When the plastic-bodied dragster came out in the 70s, everyone called them 'funny cars', due to their looks. The term flopper was born of those cars as the glassfiber body was very loose, and used to flop around.

Hardtail: A term used for a vehicle that has no rear suspension. It's ride is hard and the rear of the car is the tail.

Rollbars and rollcages: Sometimes called rollover bars by Europeans. A 'cage' of steel tubing conforming to the contours of the inside of the car. The term 'rollbar' has been substituted by lightbar or bedbar, due to legal requirements.

TWD and FWD: Two-wheel drive and 4-wheel drive (should be written as 4WD)

Wheelie bars: Located at the rear of the vehicle, these devices are located at a specific height so as to prevent a vehicle from achieving too high a vertical attitude when pulling the sled. A 'wheelie' is the act of getting the front tires high off the ground.

Wide weenies: A term used by street machine enthusiasts to indicate very wide tires, usually rear tires.

NTPA: National Tractor Pullers Assoc.

USHRA: United States Hot Rod Assoc.

NHRA: National Hot Rod Assoc.

IHRA: International Hot Rod Assoc.

SCORE: Southern California Off Road Enterprises

HDRA: High Desert Racing Assoc.

NASCAR: National Association of Stock Car Auto Racers

Principle Monster Truck Operators

Monster Truck and Puller Teams; and Sanctioning Associations

Bigfoot 4x4, Inc. & Bigfoot International Fan Club
6311 N. Lindbergh, Hazelwood, MO 63042

USA-1 4x4
c/o Off-Road Specialties
1625 N.E. Hwy 10, Spring Lake Park, MN 55432

Bear Foot, Inc.
P.O. Box 1267, Granite City, IL 62040

Awesome Kong
c/o Big Wheel Performance & Offroad Center
4015 E. Business 190, Kileen, TX 76543

Skoal Bandits & Copenhagen Crusher
c/o Golden State Promotions
618 E, Gutierrez St., Santa Barbara, CA 93103

Eagle and All-American
Spikers 4-Wheel Drive, Inc.,
814 N. Florida Ave., Lakeland FL 33801

Holman's Beast
5816 Milo Rd., Dayton OH 45414

Fly-N-Hi Toyota
Fly N-Hi Offroad
3319 W. McDowell Rd., Phoenix AZ 85009

Santanimal Wheelstander
Santana Trucking
P.O. Box 2255, Redmond WA 98052

Arfons Pulling Team
2396 Pickle Rd., Akron, OH 44312

SRO/Pace Promotions
United States Hot Rod Association
590 W. Grand Ave., Suite-C, Hot Springs, AK 71901

National Tractor Pullers Association, Inc.
Suite L-1000
6969 Worthington-Galena Rd.,
Worthington, OH 43085